Reflections
THE ART OF ALISON KINNAIRD

Introduction

ALISON KINNAIRD is one of the world's leading glass engravers. She has developed the medium by perfecting old and pioneering new techniques and has produced a very varied range of beautiful and thoughtful work that has taken glass engraving to a new level. The human form has always been an inspiration to her. Very often it has been her subject. So she was the obvious choice to design and make the Donor Window to commemorate the reopening in December 2011 of the Scottish National Portrait Gallery. It was a difficult commission. Alison was asked to create a large and complex window which would celebrate the individuals and charitable foundations that had contributed money towards the Gallery's restoration. She was asked to look at the stained glass window that had been commissioned by the Society of Antiquaries of Scotland which had been installed over a hundred years earlier at the top of the eastern staircase, alongside the position allocated to her.

The Antiquaries' Window had been designed by the Portrait Gallery's architect Sir Robert Rowand Anderson and executed by W Graham Boss. It contained small portrait roundels of the office bearers of the Society surmounted with the royal arms and the Society's arms and with the portrait of Queen Victoria at its apex. In the bottom right hand corner is the allegorical figure of summer and the date the window was installed, 15 August 1891. In discussions with Alison we agreed that the same basic pattern should be followed for the new window. There should be portrait roundels of the principal donors surrounded with garlands of flowers and name plates. Where a donor was unwilling to be represented then they could choose a bouquet of flowers. At the apex would be a portrait of our present Queen and below the insignias of the Scottish Government and the Heritage Lottery Fund, the project's two largest donors. In the bottom right hand corner would be the allegorical figure of winter and the date of the re-opening of the Gallery, 1 December 2011. It was Alison who had the inspired idea to recognise all the many lesser donors to the Gallery's renaissance in a swirl of blue figures that runs right through the window and of course it was Alison who drew the portraits and engraved them with such consummate subtlety on glass. She was assisted by Patrick Ross Smith from Shetland with whom she had worked at Dornoch Cathedral and elsewhere. The project ran unbelievably smoothly. The donors enjoyed their outings to Alison's studio at Temple. We all enjoyed selecting flowers appropriate to the individuals, and the window has been very well received by the public. It was the only work of art specifically commissioned for the new Portrait Gallery.

One of the reasons I selected Alison was my happy experience of commissioning a portrait in glass from her of the naturalist Roy Dennis. That was in 2003. It was highly original and most successful. But perhaps more important was her earlier involvement with the completion of the decoration of Mount Stuart, the great Victorian country House that was the creation of that polymath, multi-millionaire and eccentric the 3rd Marquess of Bute. Lord Bute had chosen Sir Robert Rowand Anderson to build Mount Stuart and was instrumental in getting him selected for the commission to build the Portrait Gallery. Indeed, architecturally, the two buildings are very closely related. The 3rd Marquess was one of the founding fathers of the Portrait Gallery and is represented on the earlier window. His great grandson, John, 6th Marquess was for many years Chairman of the Portrait Gallery's Advisory Committee. He had noticed and admired Alison's work when it was shown at the Scottish Gallery in Edinburgh in the late 1980s. From that encounter emerged two important commissions for Mount Stuart: One for the Horoscope Room, where Alison made panels of the four seasons including appropriate flowers and musicians; the other for a flower screen in Lord Bute's office. Another ancestor, the 3rd Earl, was not just the Prime Minister in the early 1760s but had been a noted botanist. The flowers chosen for the screen were those that grew wild on Bute. Alison worked closely with the Professor of Botany at the University of Glasgow to make sure that her designs were botanically accurate. Her inspired work at Mount Stuart was thoroughly contemporary, yet in harmony with the older building. So too was her Donor window for the Portrait Gallery. It is her greatest achievement to date.

James Holloway CBE
Director, Scottish National Portrait Gallery
1997 – 2012

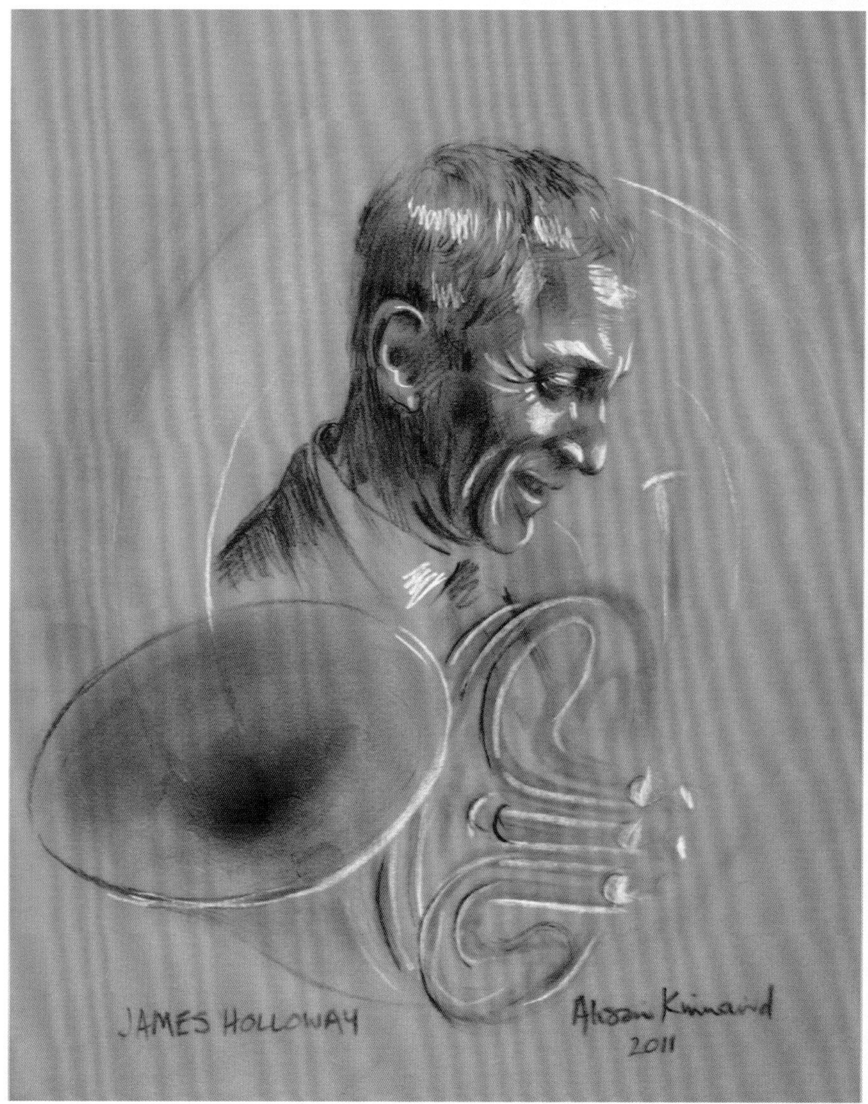

GLASS is a sublimely surprising medium. It has very special and seductive qualities. It can imitate any other medium — ceramic, metal, stone or textile — but still it has its own unique character. Glass has opposing natures - tactile but dangerous, smooth or razor-sharp, a weightless bubble, yet heavy as lead. It can reflect the observer, but it is illusory - in more than one way can one 'see through' the images engraved on its surface. Glass can be a window or a mirror; it can appear like water, ice or air. It can be colourless and ephemeral or glowing with brilliant colour. It is deceptive, adding beauty but unforgiving of error. It has a purity and a spiritual quality quite unlike any other medium.

As long as I can remember, I have drawn, painted and made things with my hands. I never expected to work with glass and became involved in wheel-engraving quite by accident. When Edinburgh College of Art did not accept me as a student, I went to Edinburgh University instead, to do a degree in Celtic Studies and Archaeology. Art was still important to me, however, and I kept up with my own artistic activities.

My father's family comes originally from Forres, near Inverness, and during a visit there, on a wet day, we happened to call in at the studio of a local craftsman, Harold Gordon, a fine copper-wheel engraver. He saw some drawings that I had been doing, and suggested that I might work with him over the summer. I was immediately hooked on the technique and the beautiful effects that are possible with wheel-engraving. During the following year, I practiced by calling in to Edinburgh Art College and getting permission to use the lathes there on an informal and occasional basis.

After I left University, I set up on my own as a copper-wheel engraver, beginning with small commissions and building up work by word of mouth.

Wheel-engraving is done with a small lathe that turns spindles with copper wheels on the end. Each wheel makes a different cut, and the engraver learns to blend these together into a design, holding the glass to touch the wheel from below. The technique of wheel-engraving is basically unchanged since Roman times. It is an old tradition, often used in a small-scale, rather classical way. I have no problem with tradition — I have always seen it as a moving point, which in many ways is also truly contemporary. Perhaps this comes from being involved for most of my life in Scottish traditional music. I have played the Scottish harp since my early teens, and my musical career as a performer, teacher and researcher has always run parallel to my art. In Scotland today, there is a vibrant and energetic approach to a musical heritage. It does not stand still, but musicians are expected to have absorbed the stylistic background and the technical skills, so that they can then be creative and personally expressive while remaining respectful of their cultural heritage. In my own case, I think that this experience has formed my approach to engraving. If a technique has survived for 2000 years, there must be something special about it The slow acquisition of wheel-engraving skills, up to the point where technique is subordinate to the idea, has been a painstaking, sometimes frustrating, but ultimately rewarding pursuit.

Engraving has an intrinsic beauty. It is difficult to make an ugly cut, though the word 'cut' itself suggests a crude and cruel process. The techniques of cold-working, of which there are many — wheel-engraving, cutting and etching, drill, diamond-point or sand-blasting — all involve breaking the surface of the glass. The choices are numerous. The medium is beautiful. The techniques produce results which are almost invariably intriguing and pleasing. The danger in all this beauty is that whatever one produces will be simply decorative. Beauty easily subsides into prettiness, and that ultimately, is cloying for artist and audience. I find that the challenge, as an artist engraving on glass, is to achieve work which is strong visually, challenging intellectually, and satisfying emotionally. I am often asked if there are any connections between the harp and the engraving. I have usually kept the two strands quite separate, apart from a couple of important projects where my art and music were directly linked. But I think that the main similarity is that both harp music and engraved glass are exquisite, apparently delicate forms of expression, in which one has to work hard to demonstrate ideas which have relevance, clarity and strength.

I usually choose the human figure as a subject. Many artists are inspired by nature, and produce lovely work. In using the human figure, I try to say something that others can relate to — to express a feeling visually. For many years, I did not clothe the figures. No style of clothing looked right — modern clothes tied the subject to a specific fashion, soon dated. Classical draperies looked 'classical'. The figures remained obstinately naked. For me, this gives a timelessness and a universality to the subjects, and

allows them to represent common feelings and tensions. The purity of the glass itself lessens the sexual element, although the naked figures are often deeply modelled. Over the years, I have done a great deal of anatomical drawing — essential to understand what is going on under the surface, because wheel-engraving is working in three-dimensions, a low-relief sculpture. It was only when I began using integral lighting and combined engraving techniques, that I found a way of depicting clothing that is effective and appropriate for my chosen subjects.

Certain themes occur again and again in my work. I often feel that the images are trapped within the glass, and that it is my job to free them. So doors and windows feature frequently. Sometimes the figures can find their way through them, and sometimes they are lost in reflections or a confusing maze. Human relationships also recur. The glass can be a mirror on these, can examine them as if through a lens, or can layer the images in the same way that we meet and pass through each others lives. Glass has the ability to be constantly shifting, or to freeze a moment in time.

I have always been interested in myth and legend from my own Scottish background, but also from other countries such as Greece and Japan. I am fascinated by the way these stories are used as metaphors for important emotions, relationships and experiences which are common to all humans. They can be read on several levels — as charming stories for children; or as much darker, deeper representa-

tions of universal truths, distilled over thousands of years. I love the use of symbols, and often use them in my work, though they may not even be recognised by a viewer - or myself - on a conscious level.

It is true that engraving is usually small-scale, and this can indeed be a problem in today's art world. Big is seen as beautiful, and work can sometimes go almost unnoticed when it is quiet and intimate. In wheel- engraving, one is limited in the size of glass on which you can engrave, by the length of the spindle to the lathe — if the glass is larger than about 40cm, you will not be able to reach the centre with the engraving wheel. You could of course use flexible drive, but copper-wheel engraving has a jewel-like quality and a subtlety of surface which is not possible with any other technique. I rather resented the fact that one was pushed to produce bigger work. When people saw an image of a piece, I was quite pleased if they found it difficult to tell the scale of the block or panel that I was working on. They often assumed that it was many times larger than the actual size. For many years I was happy to work within the constraints of the technique, and indeed, determined to embrace the precision and intimacy as part of its special character, trying to find strong subjects which did not depend on scale for their impact.

A major change in my work occurred in 2002. I was fortunate to be given a Creative Scotland Award by the Scottish Arts Council. These awards allowed an established practitioner in any of the arts to complete a proposed project. The artist was given a great deal of freedom in carrying out their ideas. Many artists found that the project evolved considerably as they went through the process, as I myself discovered. My proposal was for a work which would combine music and glass, the two strands of my career. I also wanted to incorporate light within the glass itself.

As any glass artist knows — especially engravers — light is essential in bringing the work alive. My experience is that some galleries and museums find it difficult to light the work effectively. So to a certain extent, my intention was that of self-defence — when my work went on show, I would know that it would be seen the way I wanted it to be seen. In the process of experimenting, first with optical fibre lighting, and subsequently with LEDs, I discovered that lights have huge artistic potential, as well as the obvious practical purpose of built-in illumination.

The Creative Scotland Award effectively gave me a year to experiment, and the work that I produced was 'Psalmsong', which integrated glass, music, optical fibre lighting, photography and digital printing on textile. One of the main changes was in the scale of the work. By layering sheets of optical glass, and using multiple elements, the finished length of 'Psalmsong' was more than 3 metres. I have since created work up to 8 metres long. Working on a larger scale allowed me to treat the engraving itself in a different way. I found that by painting the design with a resist, sandblasting it and then

wheel-engraving over this to define modelling and texture, I was able to be more painterly and impressionistic in the interpretation — not every detail has to be included. It also allowed me to represent new elements such as clothing effectively. I still love the slow, meditative pursuit of perfection that is intaglio engraving, but it is a tremendous relief sometimes to be allowed to loosen up, to be sketchy and free. On the first occasion that 'Psalmsong' went on display, it was seen by the Director of the Victoria and Albert Museum in London. I was immediately asked to loan it to the V&A, where it was exhibited for a year. After this, it was bought by the Scottish Parliament, and is on permanent display within the Parliament building in Edinburgh.

The first few pieces that I made with these new engraving techniques and using edge-lighting, had incorporated optical fibre lights, but I quickly found that there were practical problems of hiding the light-source, and having to dismantle the work to move it. LEDs proved to be a neater solution with enormous potential as the technology moves on. After years of engraving small, quiet, exacting pieces, the option of working up to an architectural scale, and of using the brilliant, eye-catching colour and light within the glass, has proved to be very liberating. I have to thank my husband, Robin Morton, for his technical assistance and creative input with these projects and their development over many years. With his collaboration, we have developed an effective 'turnkey' system of presenting the works, which show and travel well to exhibitions at home

and abroad. The lit installations have also attracted a great deal of international attention and interesting commissions.

Commissions have always been an important side of my work. Some artists prefer not to have direct contact with their public, but I enjoy the discussion that surrounds a potential commission. Commissions often fulfill a particular purpose, and therefore progress from a different starting-point. They push you to take on subjects that you might not normally choose and stretch the imagination and technique in order to satisfy both the client and the artist. Sometimes they have to include specific information, and sometimes they have to fit into an architectural situation where a defined space or the constraints of working within a historic building must be taken into account. I have been fortunate to have been asked to make work for the homes of private individuals, for modern projects such as a hotel in the United States and a church in Edinburgh, as well as historic institutions such as a 14th century Cathedral and the Scottish National Portrait Gallery, where my glass is now a permanent part of these important buildings. I also enjoy being asked to make smaller, personal commissioned pieces for individuals who wish to mark a particular occasion, or simply to own a piece which has been specially executed for them.

As I developed my skills to the point where expressing my ideas did not depend on technique, and was able to work on more interesting forms of glass,

sometimes specially made for me,
exhibitions gradually became a more
significant part of my links with an
audience. When works go on show, it is
fascinating and sometimes moving to see
how the viewers respond to them,
sometimes in a very emotional way.
It is always interesting to hear what they
read into the work, often bringing out
layers of meaning that I had not consciously
realised were there. One also values the
contributions of writers who are
knowledgeable commentators on
the contemporary scene, some of
whom have kindly allowed me to
include quotes in this book..

After forty years of working with a
medium that may be seen as limiting,
I have never come to the end of possibilities.
Intaglio and relief engraving with copper or
diamond wheels; cameo glass or glass
flashed with colour; three-dimensional
pieces or flat panels. But most importantly,
the subjects which suggest themselves
are constantly exciting, relevant and
absorbing, and I am looking forward
with anticipation to the years to come.

Alison Kinnaird MBE

2006

50cm h x 50cm w
x 10cm d

Optical glass,
sandblast and
wheel-engraved,
LED lighting with
dichroic colour.

Fitzwilliam Museum,
Cambridge.

Photo: Robin Morton

SELF-PORTRAIT

This portrait was a commission for presentation to the Museum which was instigated
by John Keatley, for many years a great supporter of the Guild of Glass Engravers.
A self-portrait is always an interesting exercise. Here I show the two sides of my
activities, on the right, playing the Scottish harp, and on the left, making my mark,
as an engraver. The interlacing patterns are 'lissajous' patterns, formed by sampling
soundwaves across the wave, so they are the visual expressions of musical notes.

SHILLINGHILL, Temple

Studio and workbench

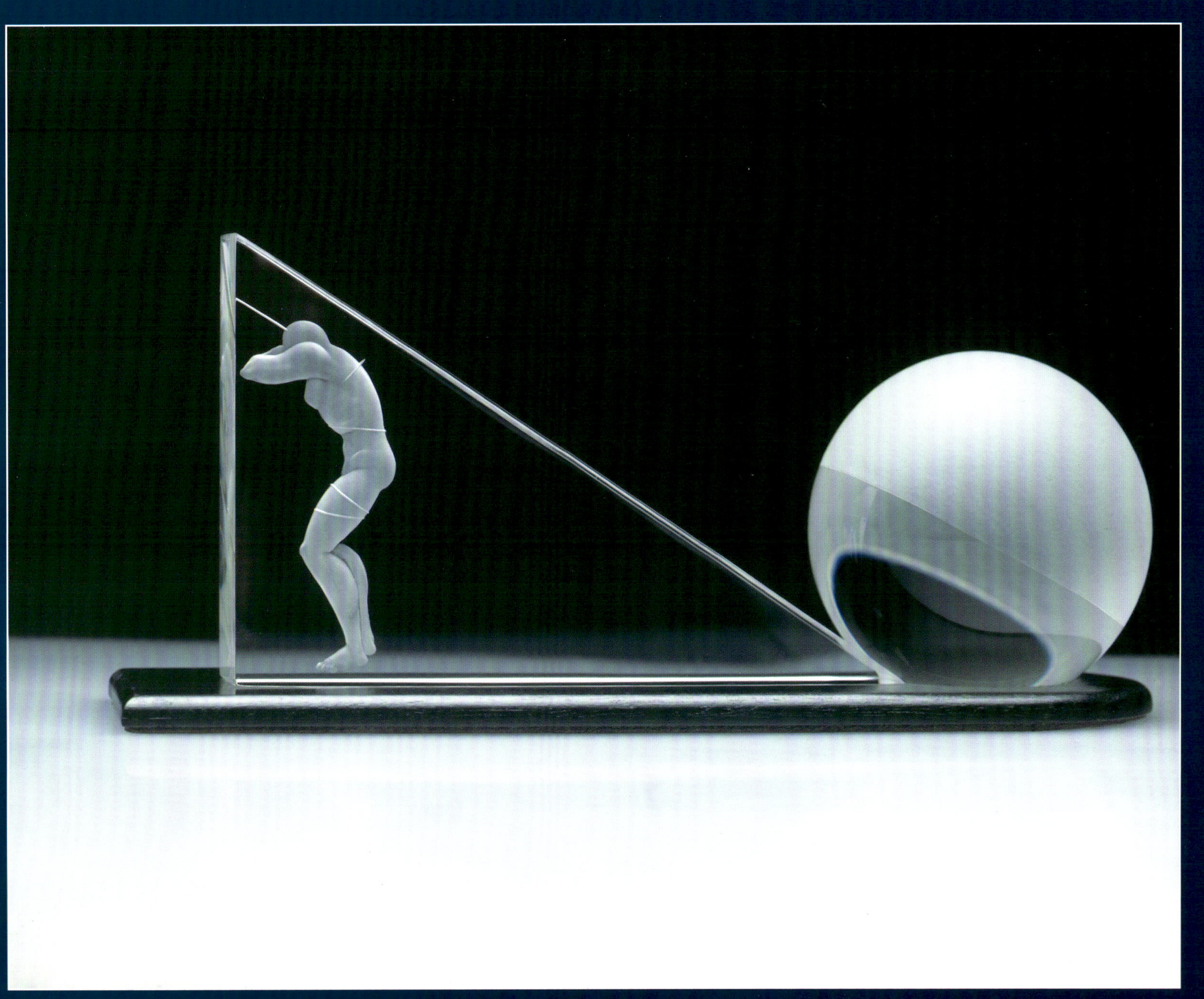

EOSTRA

The strong shape of the glass triangle traps the figure of the woman within it. It comments on the female situation. There are references to Easter, a fertility festival, when eggs are rolled down slopes, stones are rolled away from tombs, and there is rebirth – a time of life and death, emphasised by the half-frosted globe, both solid and liquid.

1995

23cm h x 32cm w x 10cm d

Optical glass, copper-wheel engraved

Private Collection

Photo: Ken Smith

HORSEMAN An installation about transformation, shape-shifting and movement. The shadow banner behind shows the actual shadows of the engraving, photographed and digitally printed on textile to form a permanent backdrop.

2005, Glass – 26cm h x 165cm w, Optical glass, sandblast and wheel-engraved, LED light with dichroic colour, printed textile, Private Collection, Photo: Robin Morton

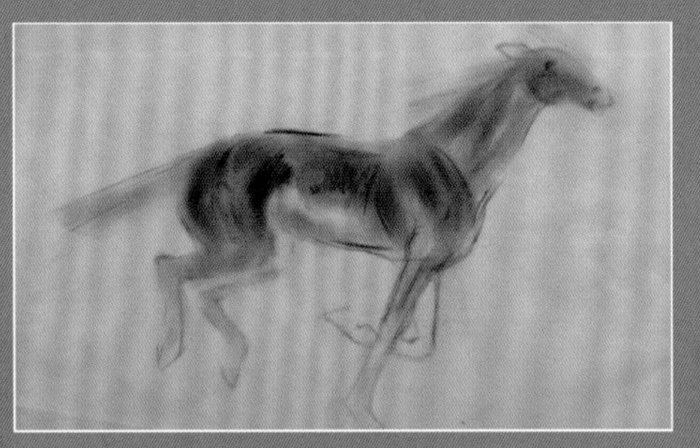 

"In the close-knit coterie of glass-engravers, Alison Kinnaird's work is exceptional in her mastery of multi-faceted, multi-layered symbolistic story-telling. The nature of the technique requires close and concentrated engagement with its audience, but once engaged, a perspective opens out in so many directions that a whole world of ancient and contemporary references are there to be read." *JENNIFER OPIE, CRAFTS, 1998*

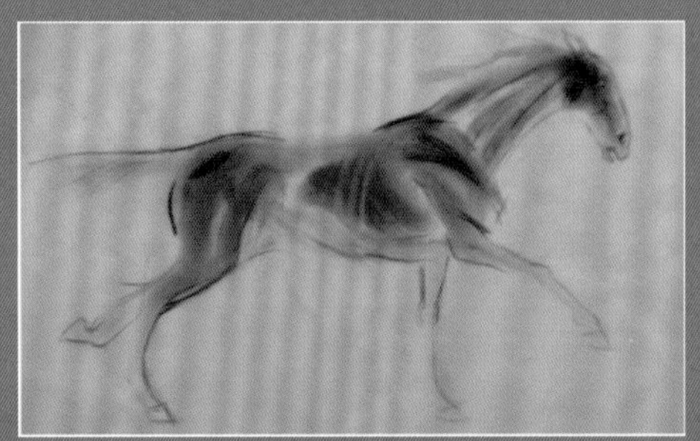 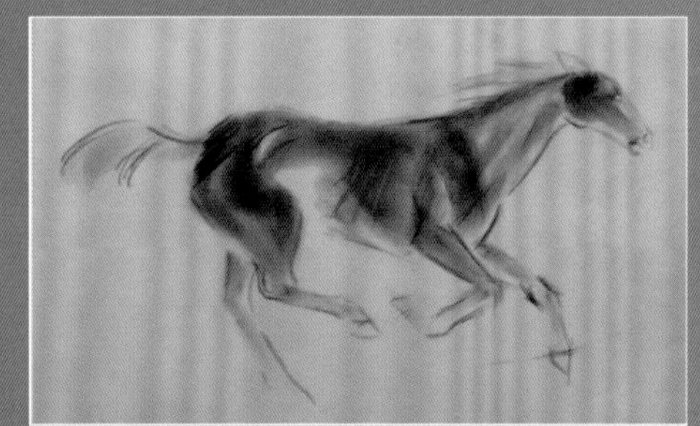

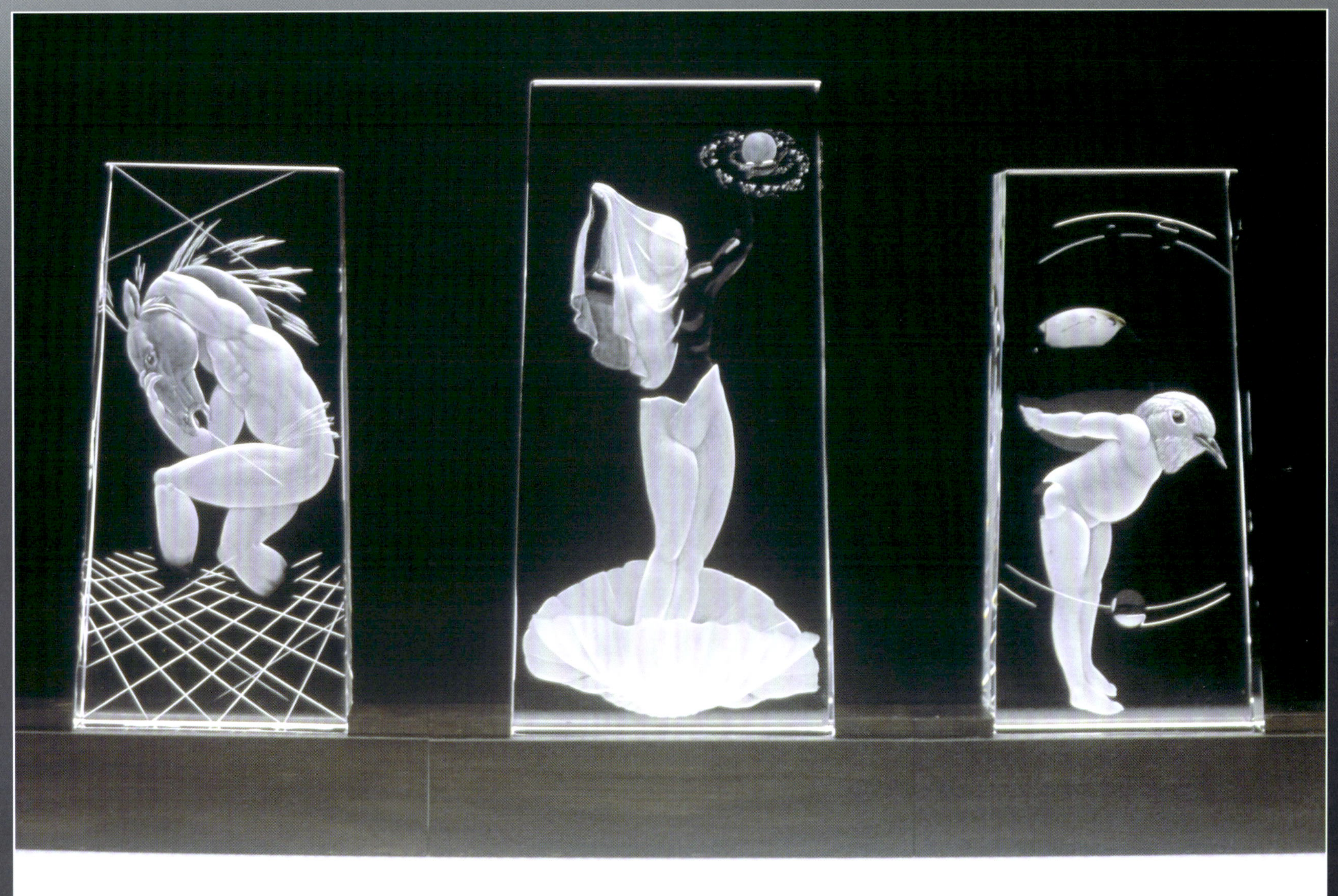

1995

23cm h x 32cm w x 10cm d

Optical glass, copper-wheel engraved

Victoria & Albert Museum

Photo: Ken Smith

TRIPTYCH Past, Present and Future, represented as Man, Woman and Child. The atavistic horse-headed male figure is trapped in the web of time. The female figure refers to Botticelli's Venus, but shows her as a shell within a shell, veiled in stars like the Celtic Madonna, 'Reul na Mara', the Star of the Sea. The Child is masked as a Wren, a bird hunted in Scotland and Ireland at New Year, and carries on its back the invisible, untouched, polished globe of the future.

MAN INTO SEAL

Glass is a material in transition, caught between solid and liquid. Shape -shifting is a common theme in Scottish legend and ballad. The clan MacCodrum is said to be descended from seals which became human when they came to land.

1989

30cm diam

Double cased crystal disc

Corning Museum of Glass, NY

Photo: Ken Smith

NARCISSUS

A treatment of the Greek legend, commissioned by a client who had studied botany in literature. The reference to the mirror pool in the story made it an ideal subject in glass.

2007

30cm h x 46cm w x 18cm d

Optical glass, sandblast and wheel-engraved, LED light Mirrored base

Private Collection

Photo: Robin Morton

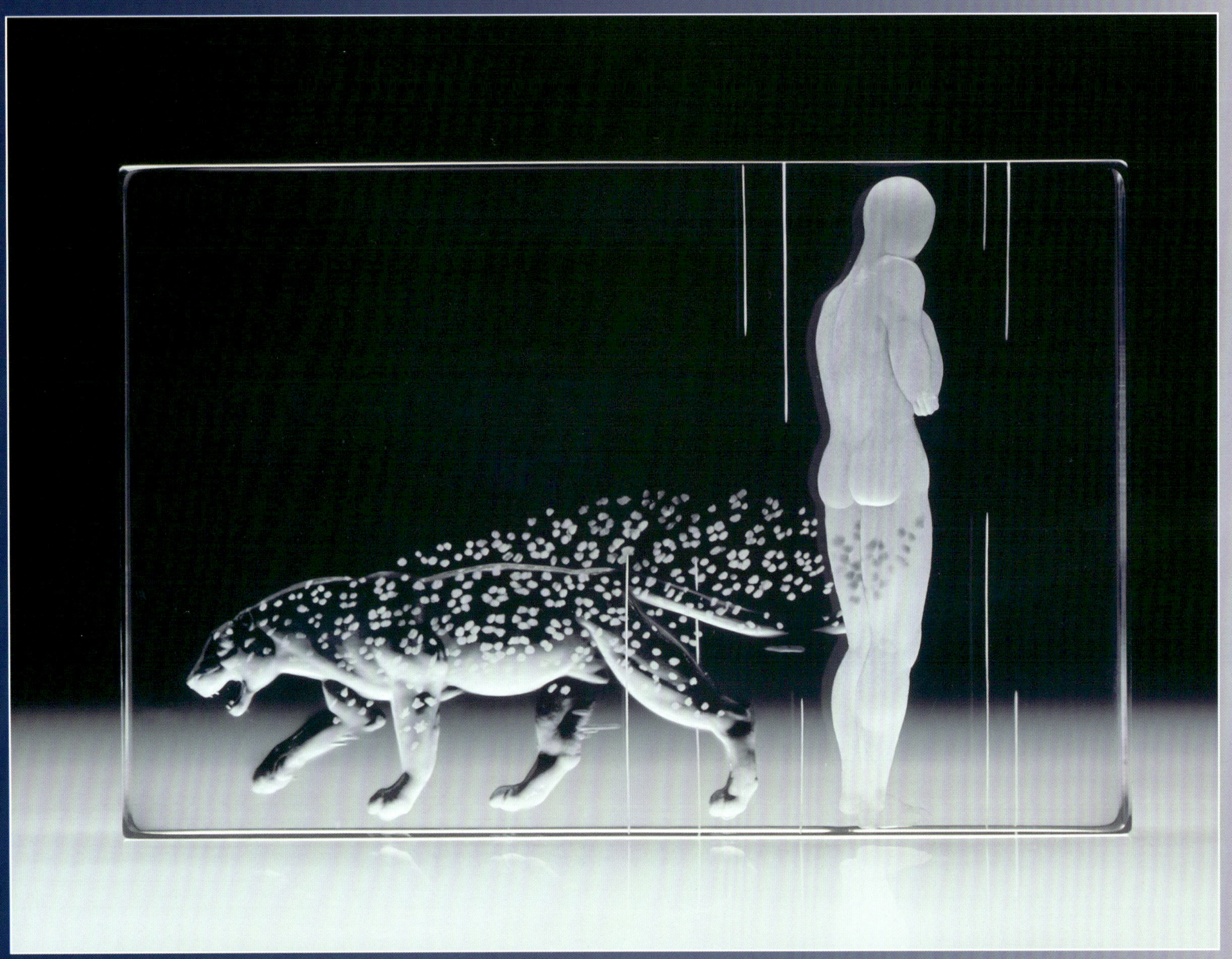

LEOPARD LADY

The illusory nature of glass is ideal for surreal effects. The leopard's spots drift off across the woman
– but can anyone really change their spots?

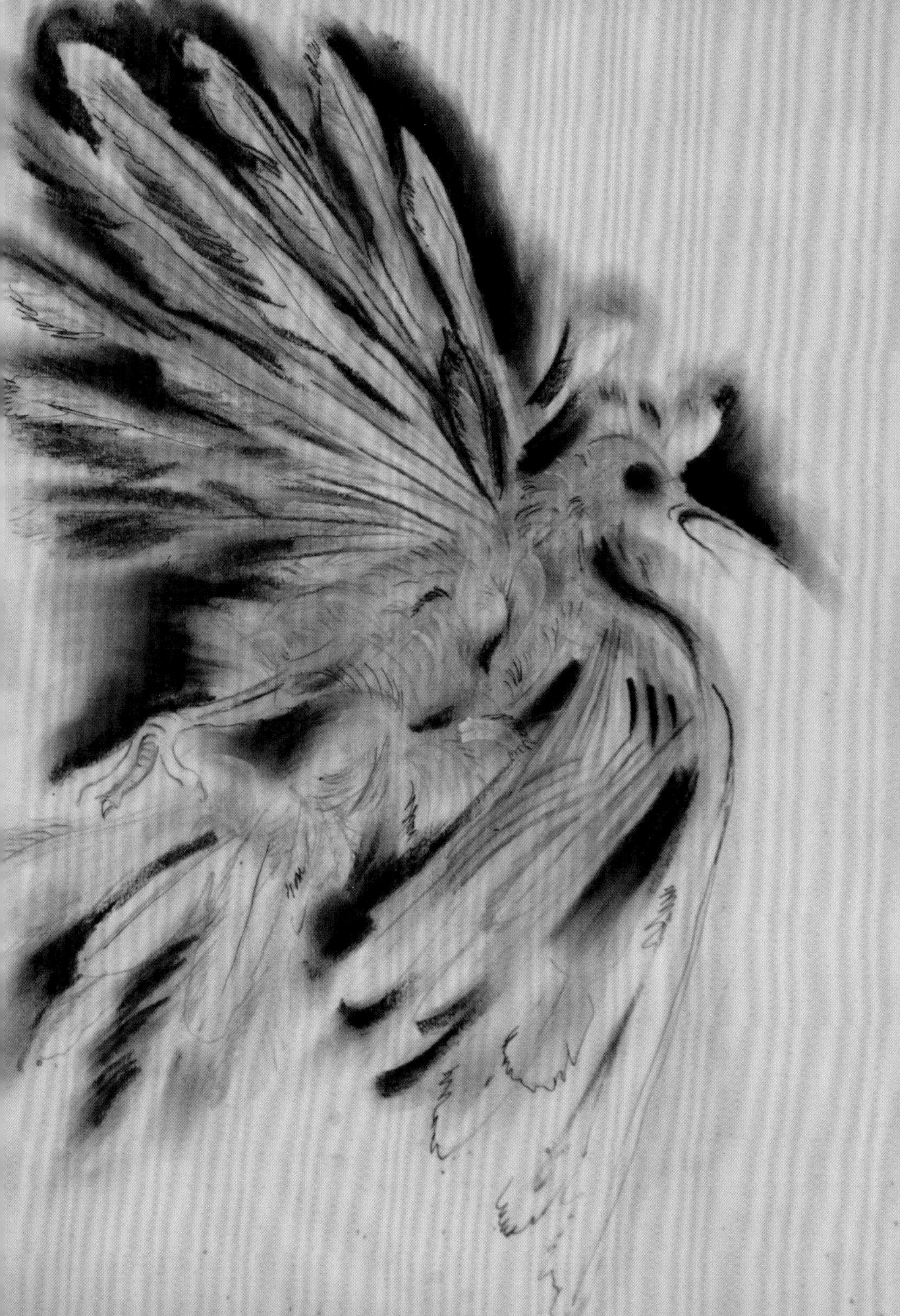

"The fusing of elements which is the essence of glass-making is an appropriate metaphor to describe Alison Kinnaird's use of glass as the medium for her art; hers is a fusing with the physical elements of glass of metaphysical elements of imagery and perceptions, inner worlds and 'otherworlds', symbolism, inherited belief and lost experience, time and timelessness."

HUGH CHEAPE, ROYAL MUSEUMS OF SCOTLAND.
THE SCOTTISH GALLERY EXHBITION CATALOGUE, 1997

WINGED BOAT

Boats can represent a cradle or a coffin, and have a special place as symbols of the journey through life.

1990

22cm h x 15cm w x 11cm d

Lead crystal, copper-wheel engraved

Private Collection

Photo: Ken Smith

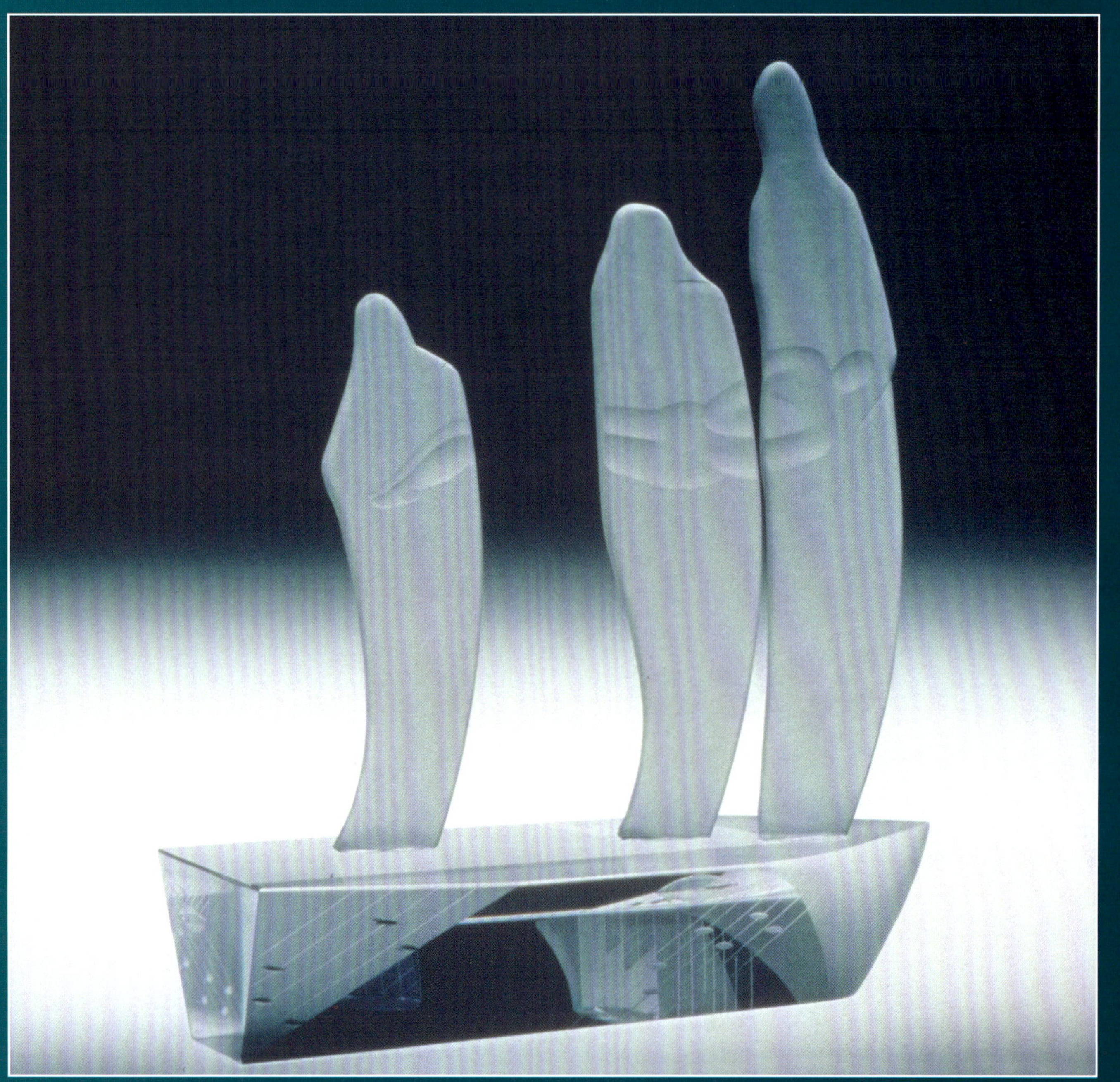

IONA

The Island of Iona has special significance in Scottish history as the burial place of the Scottish Kings. It seemed appropriate to adopt this as symbolic of the end of all our journeys.

1989

20cm h x 20cm w x 9cm d

Lead crystal, cut, wheel engraved

Private collection

Photo: Ken Smith

PSALMSONG This installation was the result of a Creative Scotland Award in 2002, and represents a watershed point in my career. The starting point was an original composition of harp music, which I based on the 'question and answer' form of Gaelic psalmsinging. I had the notes of the harp analysed at the Physics Department of Edinburgh University, and the soundwaves this created were sampled across the waves. The 'lissajous' patterns thus formed are interlacing lines, not unlike Celtic knotwork. One of these patterns was chosen to represent each note of the melody, and the music written out in this way. Human figures and colour from dichroic glass were incorporated in the design to suggest the emotional content of the music. The glass is edge-lit

with optical fibre lighting. A permanent shadow was captured by photographing the shadow of the engraving, and digitally printing it on a textile banner that hangs behind the installation. The music was recorded on gut and wire-strung harps, cello and glass, so that we hear the sound of the medium as well as seeing the visual expression of the sound.

The installation was shown a number of times in Scotland, and I was invited to show it for a year in the Victoria & Albert Museum in London. It was given the Glass Sellers Award in 2004 by the Worshipful Company of Glass Sellers of London. It is now in the permanent collection of the Scottish Parliament, and is on show in the Parliament Building in Edinburgh.

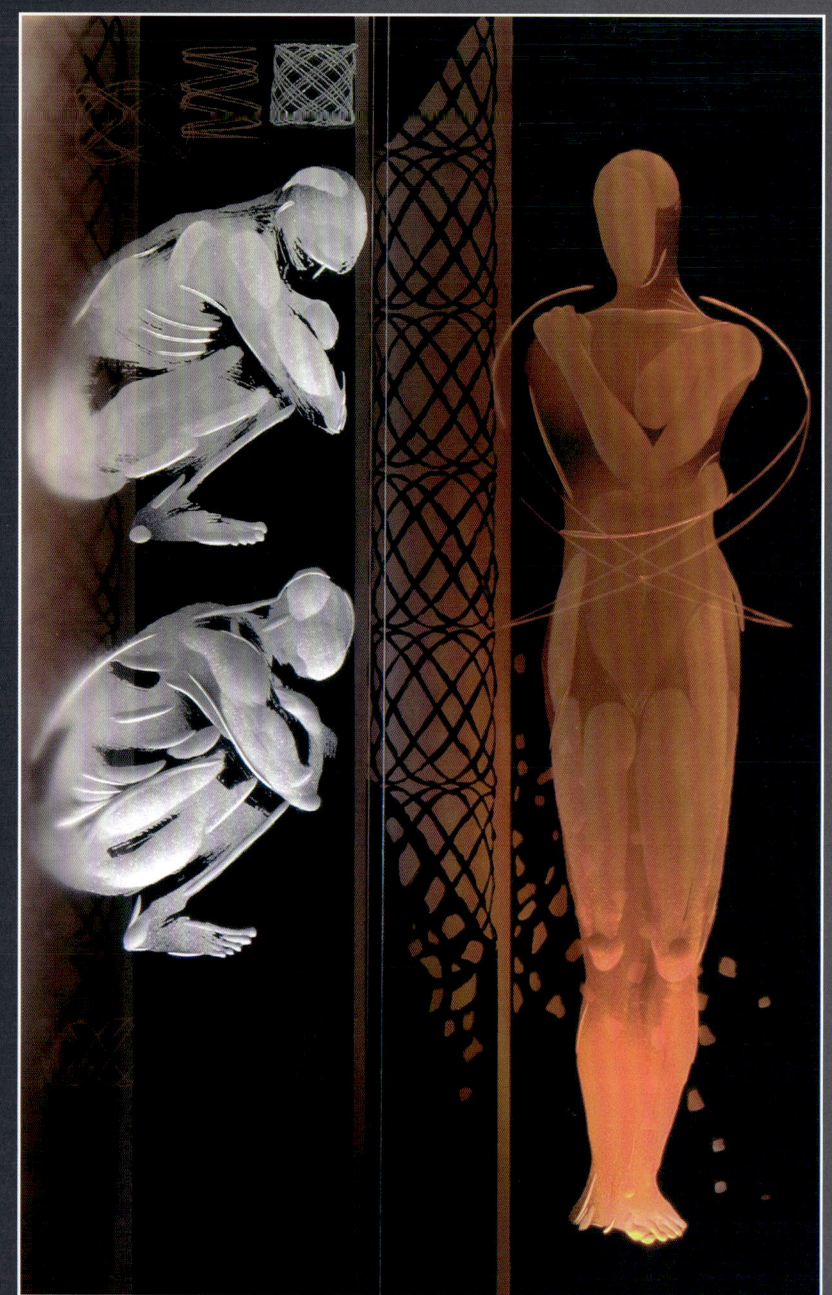

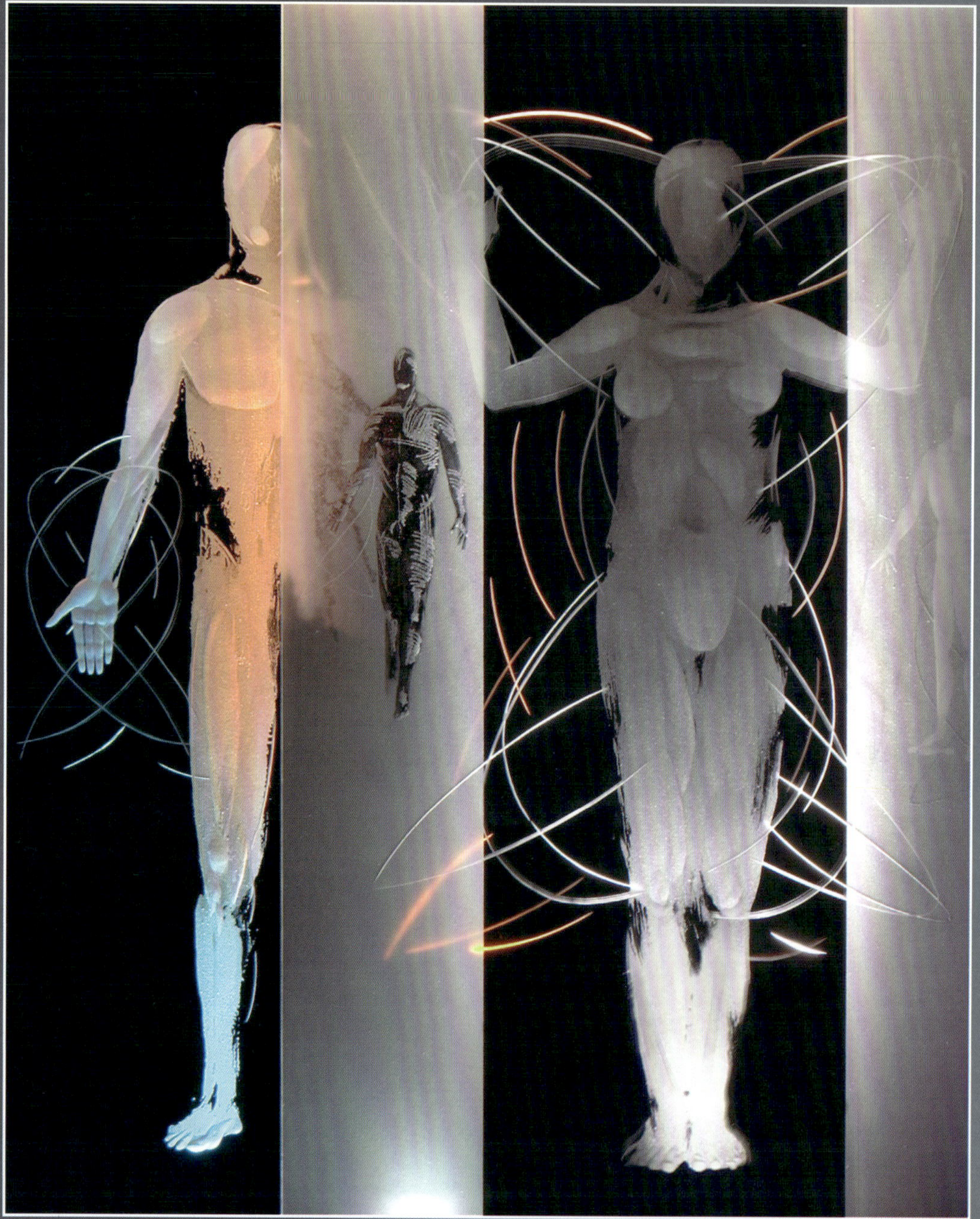

PSALMSONG details

PSALMSONG

2003

Glass – 40cm h x 330cm w,

Optical glass, sandblast and
wheel-engraved, optical fibre
lighting with dichroic colour.

Digitally printed textile.

Scottish Parliament Art Collection

Photos: Simon Hollington

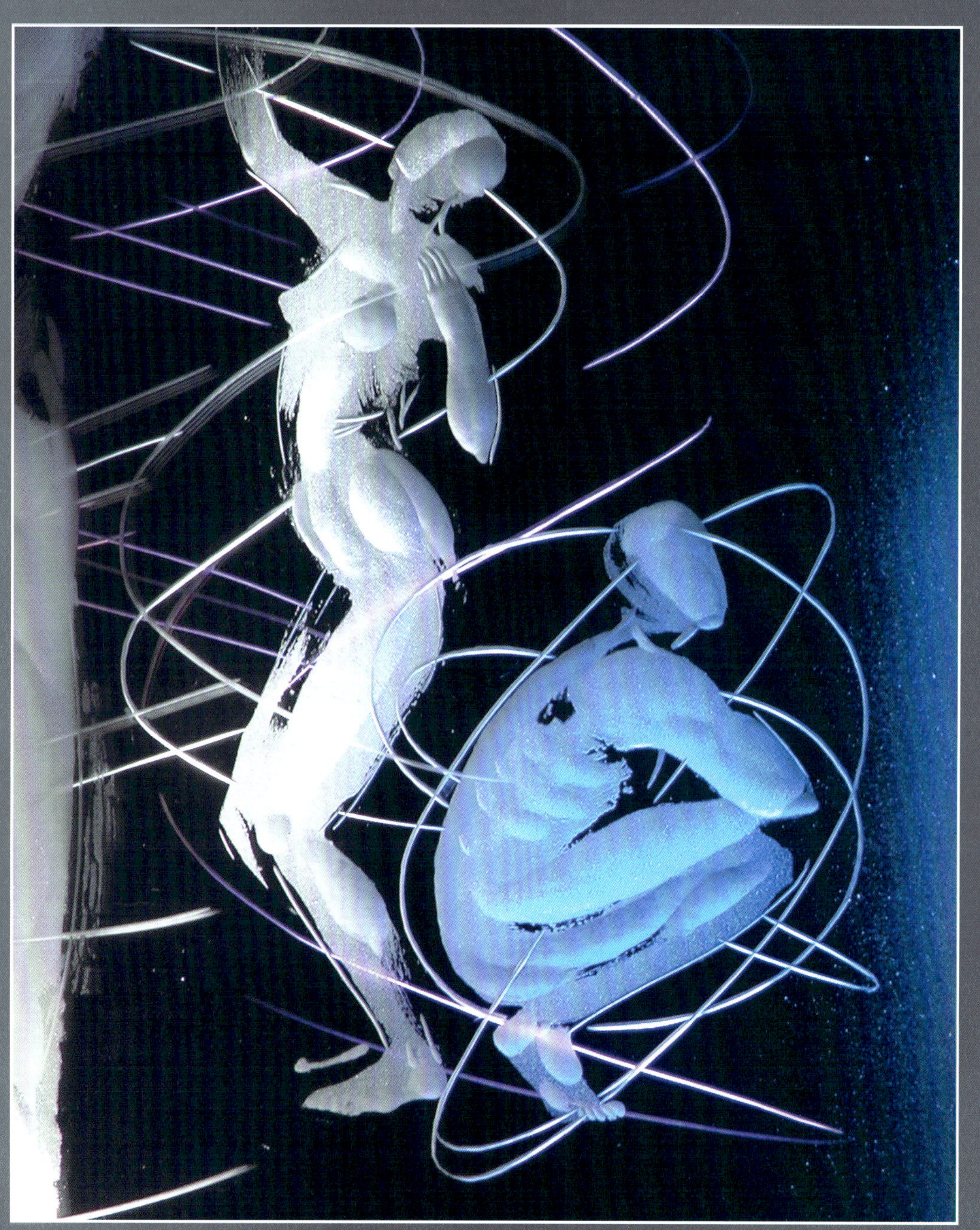

RING OF CRYSTAL, RING OF STONE

This was the first piece in which I combined music and glass. It is based on the idea of a circle of standing stones. The figures may be hidden, dismembered, split or disguised in different ways, but the human figure ultimately comes through again, both entering and leaving a doorway. The harp music that I composed to match it also follows this shape – the traditional form of Scottish harp music is a theme with variations, returning to the theme in the end.

1990

35cm h x 50cm w x 45cm d

Optical glass, wheel-engraved

Leicester Museum Collection

Photos: Ken Smith

"Framing, supplied by the form of the glass or by the scheme of the engraving, intensifies

an illusion of looking into or passing through a door, thus passing from one world into

another, an 'otherworld' of the fear or imagination or a point of confrontation,

a sensation heightened by the typically recurring motionless figure poised between, say,

history and prehistory, a known and an unknown world, and in this case not a material

world of the fervent romantic, but perhaps the being within us."

DOORS ON THE PAST

This piece was commissioned to mark the joining together of several institutions which form the Royal Museums of Scotland. The glass is treated as a doorway through which figures can pass, with references to megalithic stones. Both an end and a beginning.

1986

30cm h x 30cm w x 10cm d

Cased lead crystal disc, optical glass blocks, wheel-engraved, silver mount

Commissioned by the Royal Museums of Scotland

Photo: Ken Smith

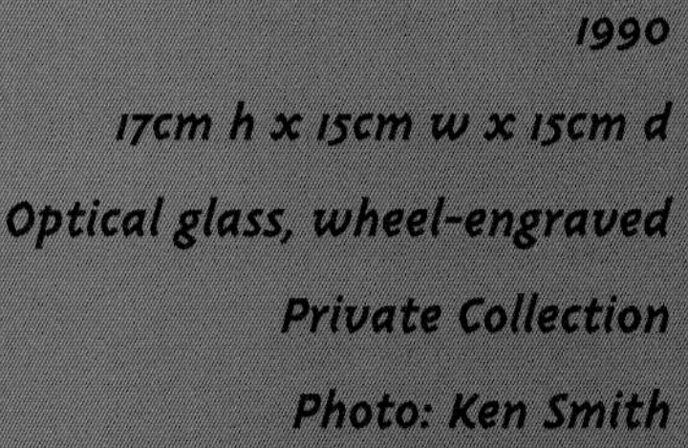

WAYS OUT

The figure is trapped within the glass
— the signs for escape appear and
disappear with the reflections as the
viewer moves round the piece.

1990

17cm h x 15cm w x 15cm d

Optical glass, wheel-engraved

Private Collection

Photo: Ken Smith

SHADOW DOOR

The shifting reflections within the glass are constantly surprising.

1985

24cm h x 16cm w x 12cm d

Lead crystal, wheel-engraved

Private Collection

Photo: Ken Smith

EXIT

This installation plays on the fact that the edge-lighting that I use in my lit panels uses the same basic principle as that used in Exit signs. It also speaks about the way that we pass through each others' lives, some knowing the direction that they are going, others following confusing signals.

2008

40cm h x 115cm w x 15cm d

Optical glass, sandblast and wheel engraved,
LED lighting with dichroic colour

Private Collection

Photo: Robin Morton

LEAP

1987
25cm diameter
Lead crystal, cased, wheel-engraved
Ulster Museum, Belfast
Photo: Ken Smith

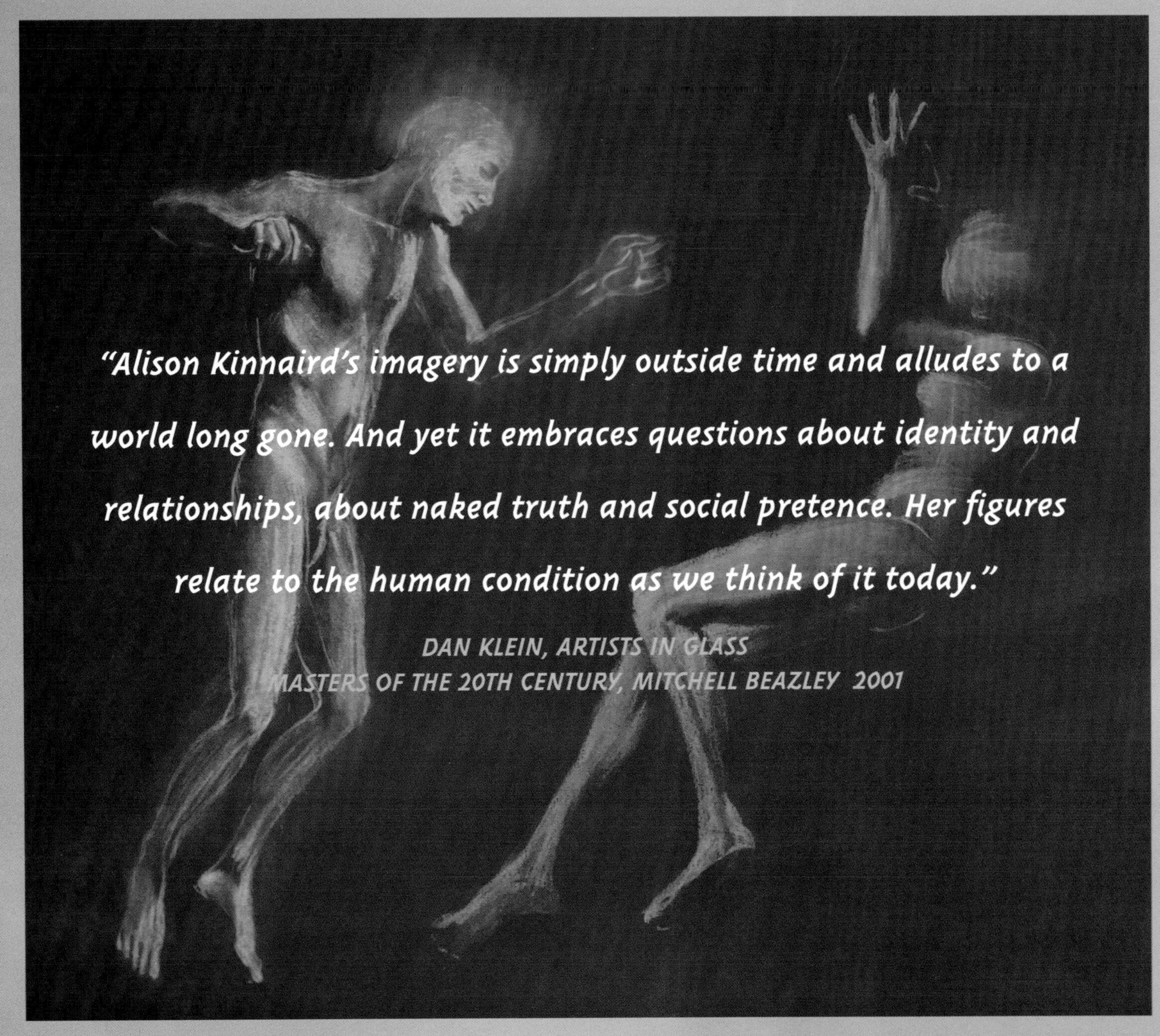
"Alison Kinnaird's imagery is simply outside time and alludes to a world long gone. And yet it embraces questions about identity and relationships, about naked truth and social pretence. Her figures relate to the human condition as we think of it today."

DAN KLEIN, ARTISTS IN GLASS
MASTERS OF THE 20TH CENTURY, MITCHELL BEAZLEY 2001

CHAIN

The contrast between the solidity of the resin and the transparency of the glass emphasises the apparent freedom of those figures in the glass, opposed to those trapped in the opaque resin. Still the figures are linked together by the chains.

2001

20cm h x 27cm w x 7cm d

Optical glass, wheel-engraved, white resin cast off the engraved glass

Private Collection

Photo: Ken Smith

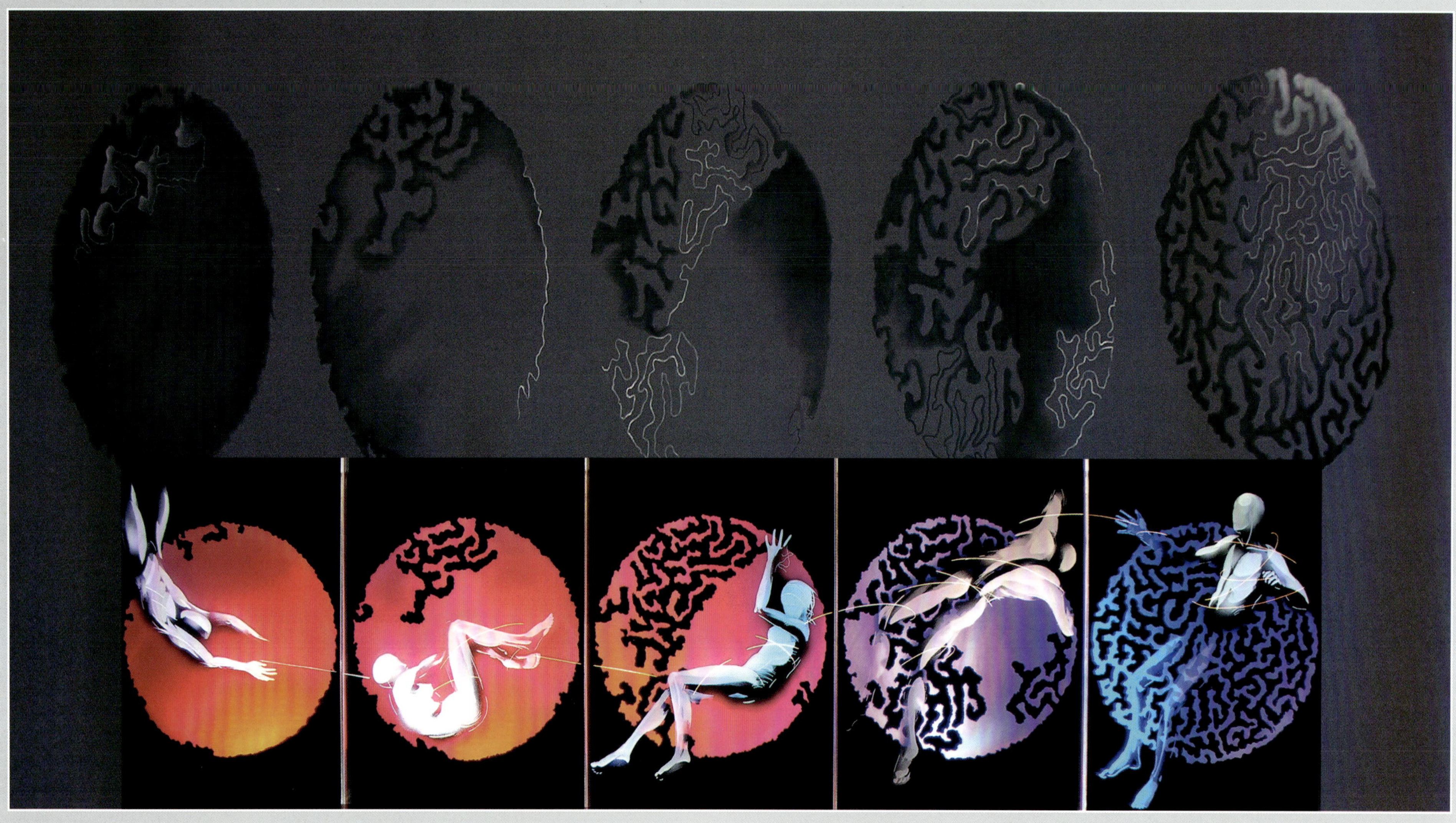

MAZE The Maze is an evocative concept in many cultures. It can represent Heaven or Hell; sometimes the aim is to reach the centre, sometimes to escape from it. It can symbolise the difficult path through life, through which a tenuous thread is the only guide. While researching on the internet, I found examples of a scientific experiment, where the natural drying process of drops of a solution containing tiny glass spheres, created mazelike patterns as the liquid crystallised. To me, the patterns symbolised both life and death, regeneration and decay, and I adapted them as the background layer of the panel, and also painted a version of them on the backdrop. The figures are tossed about in the storms of life, and tangled round them is a golden thread, which represents the line of life. This line is lit by programmed LEDs, so that it gradually appears, leading the eye through the piece.

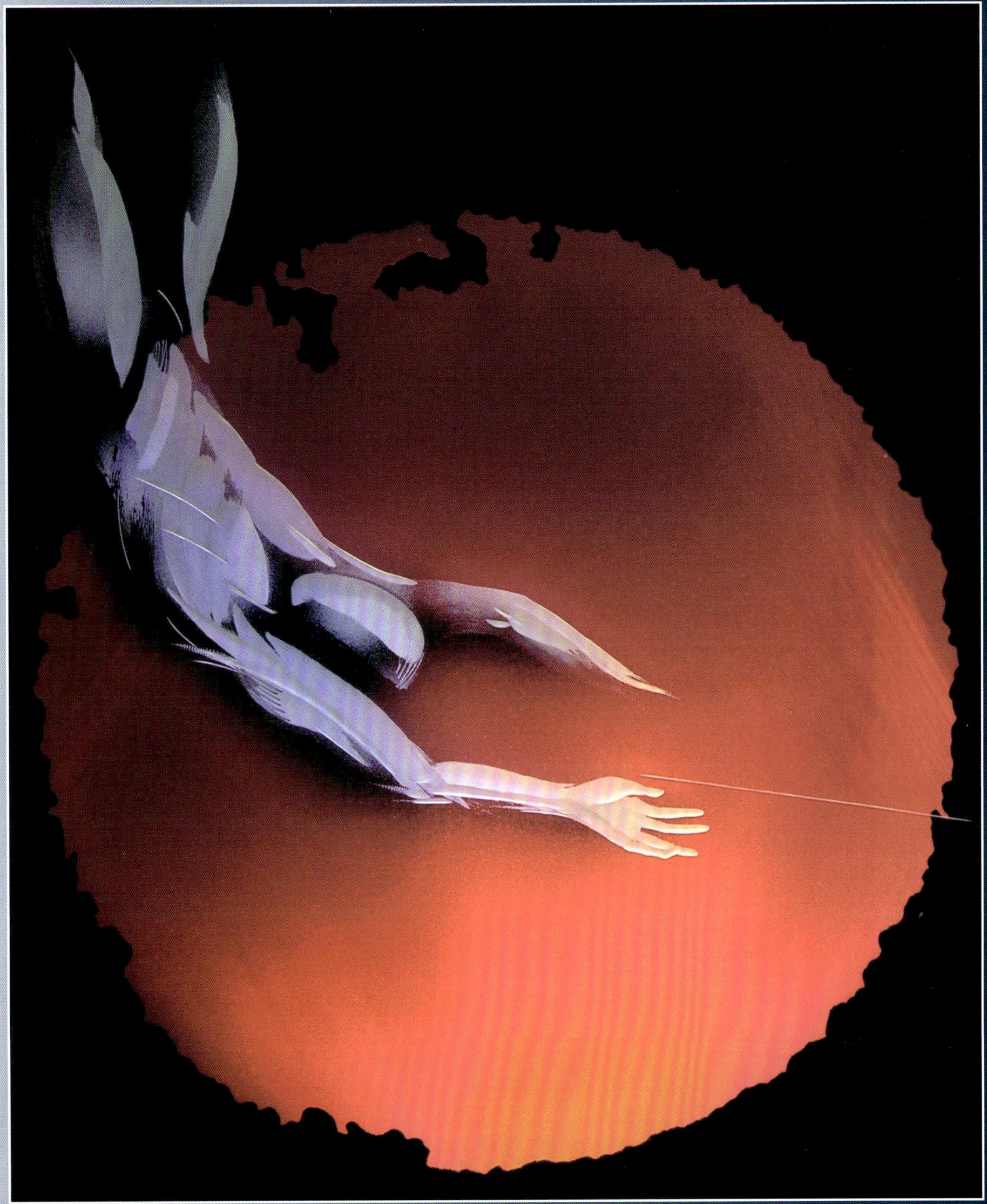

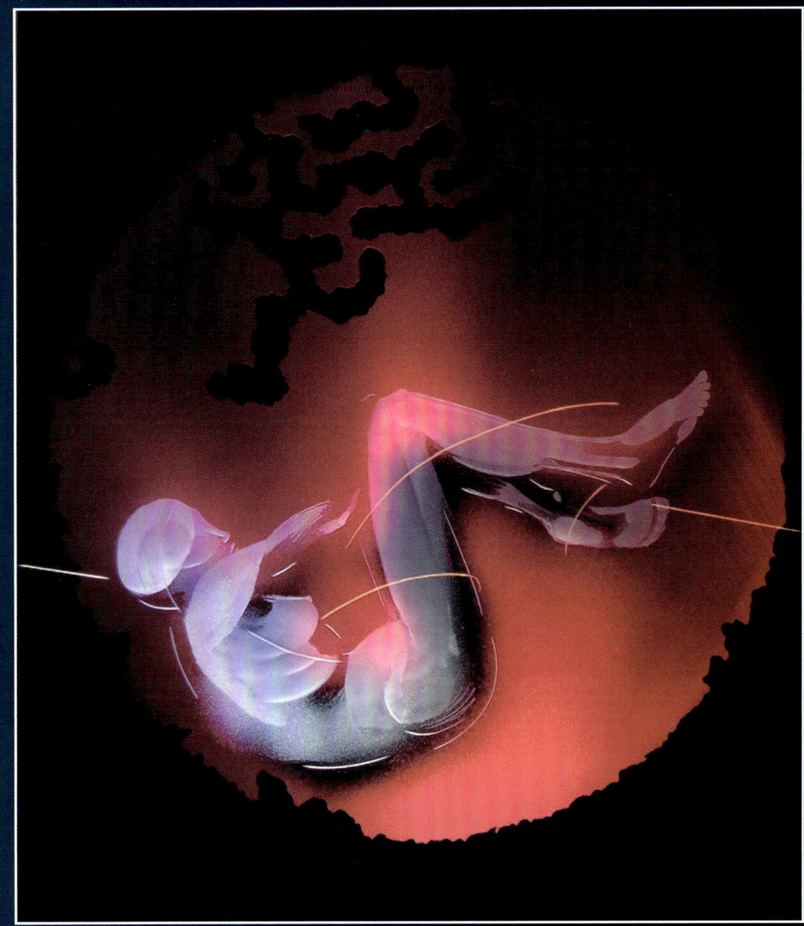

MAZE details

2007

Glass – 40cm h x 130cm w

Optical glass, sandblast and wheel-engraved, LED light with dichroic colour and moving programmed sequence, printed textile.

Commissioned by the Royal Museums of Scotland

Photos: Robin Morton

PASSING THROUGH

This piece was created for the Coburg Glaspreis
Exhibition. It was the first time that a programmed
sequence of LEDs was used, allowing the line drawn
figure on the back layer to 'walk through' the
installation, as if it were animated, and, as people
pass through each others' lives, barely noticeable.
The backdrop behind the work is printed from a
photograph of the shadow of the engraving.

2006

Glass – 40cm h x 130cm w

*Optical glass, sandblast and wheel-engraved,
LED lighting with dichroic colour and
programmed sequence*

Digitally printed textile

Morton Fraser Collection, Edinburgh

Photos: Robin Morton

PASSING THROUGH details

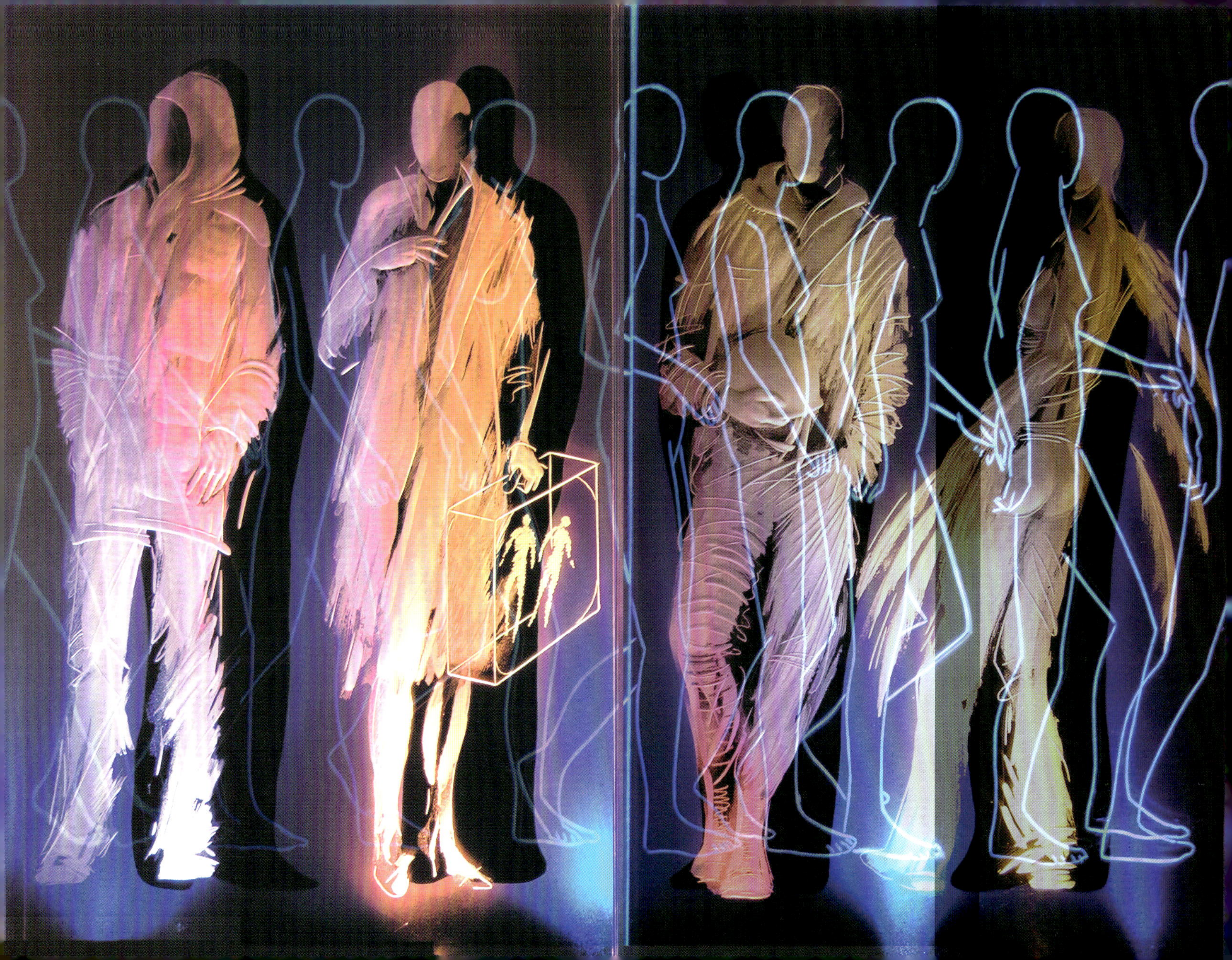

"Alison Kinnaird creates pictures based on expansive narration charged with powerful emotions. Although her glass objects are usually closed forms, the scenes carved on them seem to have the potential to be continued."

DOROTA MILKOWSKA (TRANSLATION: MACIEJ IGNACZAK)
'FOUR POINTS OF A COMPASS', WROCLAW, POLAND 2011

APARTMENT BLOCKS

This is an on-going series of optical cubes, each portraying a small domestic drama of human relationships.
The title is a play on the fact that lives are carried on quite separately within their own spaces in many city settings in modern times. The black resin blocks are each cast off the engraved surfaces, and also engraved with graffiti, a subject that I have often used in different works. The blocks can be placed individually, or stacked in different sequences into towers.

2011 – 13

Each cube 10 cm x 10cm x 10cm

Optical glass black resin

*Photo: Lutz Naumann,
Kunstsammlung der Veste Coburg*

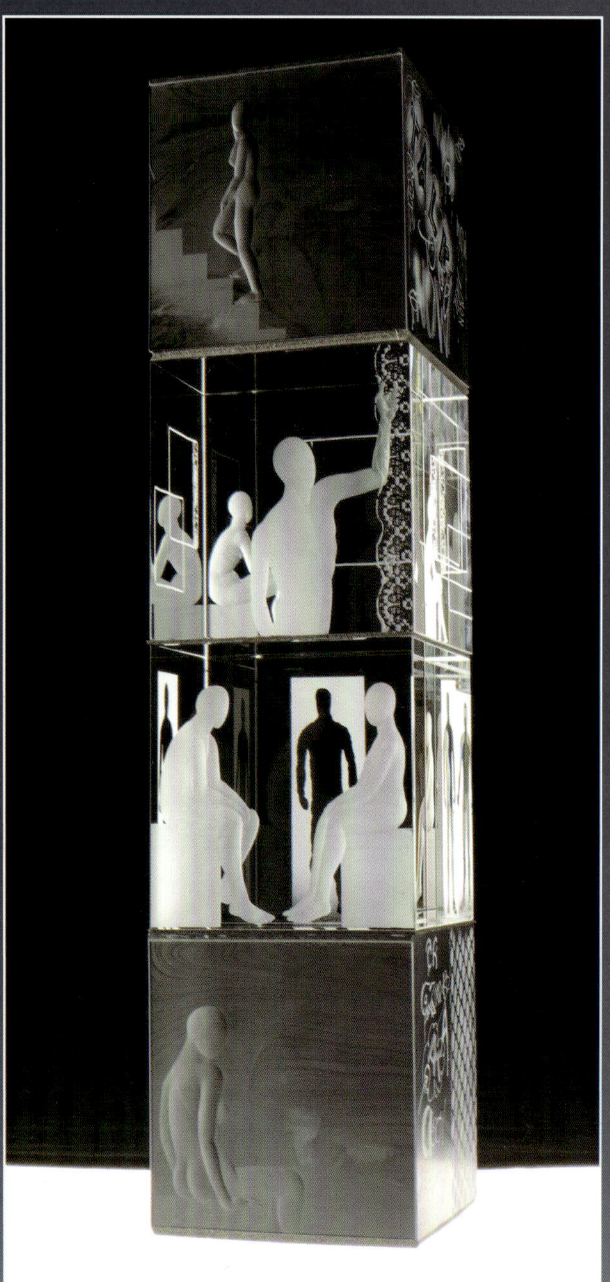

Photos: Ken Smith

APARTMENT BLOCK details

Photo © Tina Norris

STREETWISE I & II

A contemporary treatment of city life and relationships in an urban setting, exploring the possibilities of layering the panels of glass. This was the first piece in which it was clearly appropriate to clothe the figures.

2004

Glass - 50cm h x 260cm w

Optical glass, sandblast and copper-wheel engraved, optical
fibre lighting with dichroic colour. Digitally printed textile

Streetwise I – Tutsek Foundation, Munich

Streetwise II – Dundee Art Gallery and Museum

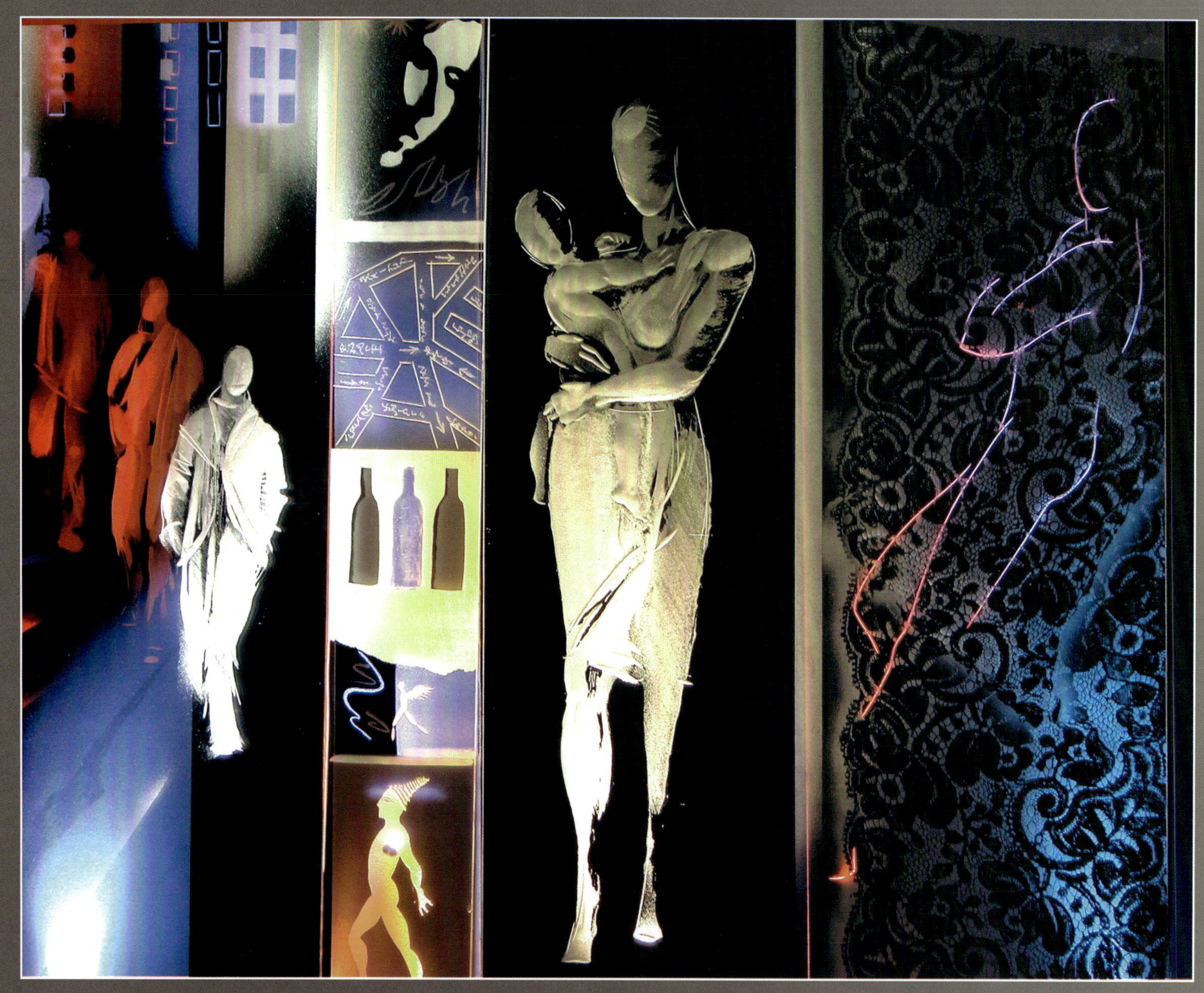

STREETWISE details

FRAGILE
GLASS
GirlS
FRAGILE

HEVSNE
FRA
GILE

STREETLIGHT & DRAWING FOR STREETLIGHT
I saw this teenager's face in a news report.
It seemed both beautiful and lonely.

2011

40cm h x 26cm w x 15cm d

Optical glass, sandblast and wheel-engraved,
LED lighting with dichroic colour

Photo: Robin Morton

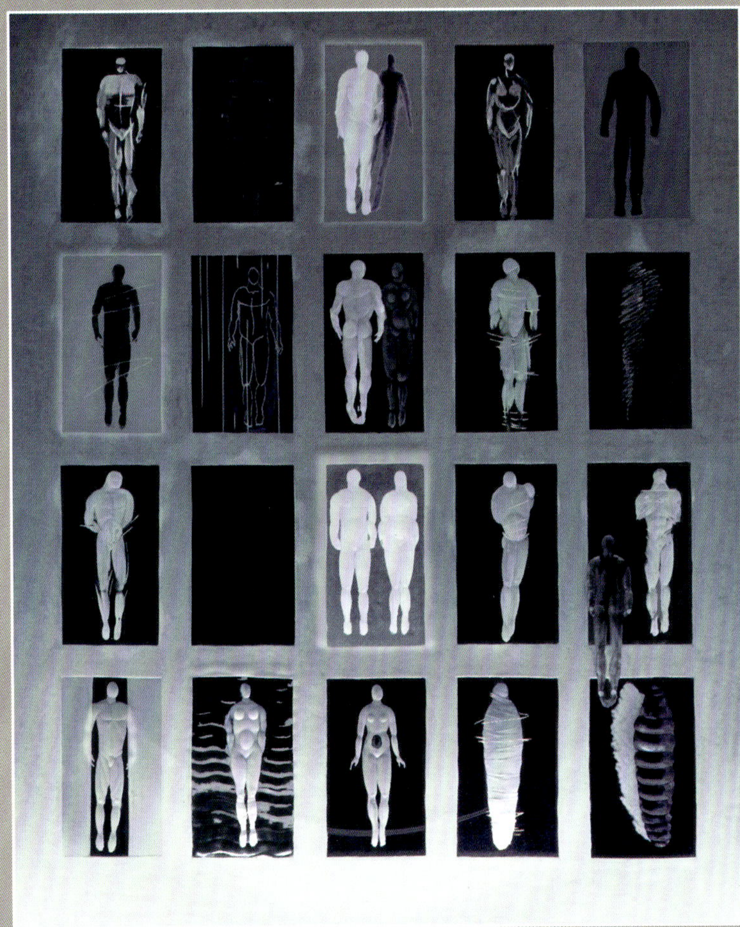

SAMPLER

This explores the many variations possible when depicting the human figure. Each unit within the design is also about the same size as a scientific microscopic slide, as contemporary society puts us all into boxes.

2004

35cm h x 26cm w x 10cm d

Lead crystal, steel mount Wheel-engraved

Dan Klein and Alan J.Poole Collection in the Royal Museums of Scotland

Photo: Ken Smith

BARCODED

Modern technology increasingly defines personalities in mechanical ways – though everyone is different, our individuality is taken away.

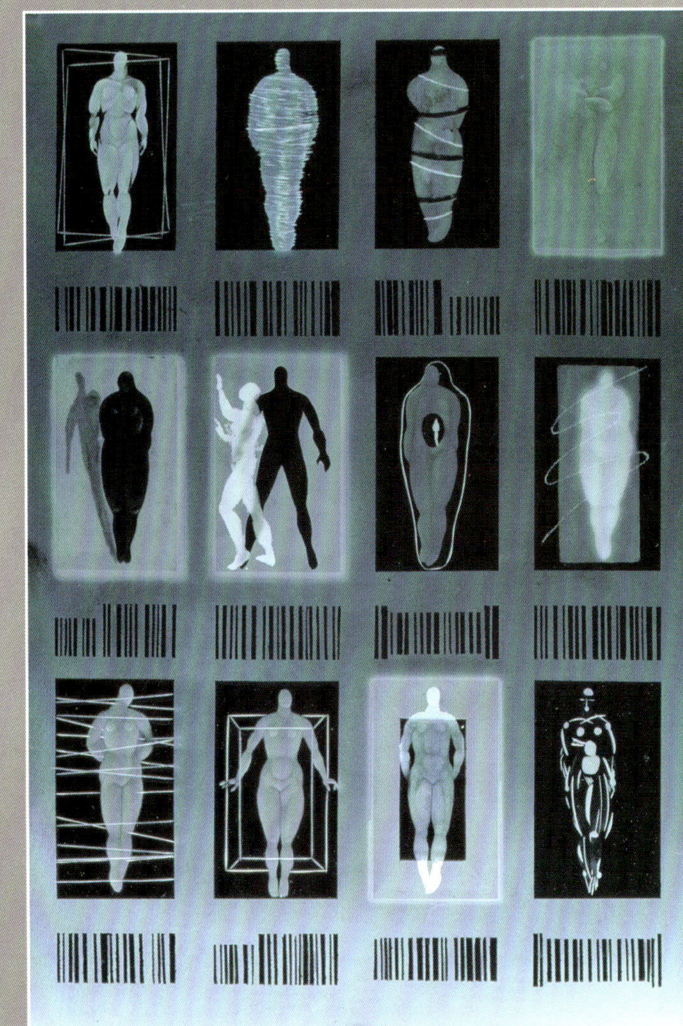

2005

35cm h x 24cm w x 10cm d

Lead crystal, steel mount Sandblast and wheel-engraved

Private Collection

Photo: Ken Smith

BLUE STUDY

2005

50cm h x 50cm w x 2cm d

*Optical glass, wheel-engraved
and sandblasted LED lighting
with dichroic colour*

Private Collection

Photo: Robin Morton

CONTRAFLOW
Most people follow the crowd, but some people go their own way.

2005

50cm h x 50 cm w x 2cm d

Optical glass, wheel-engraved and sandblasted LED lighting with dichroic colour

Private Collection

Photo: Robin Morton

FLIGHTPATH

An installation on the subject of migration – not always a happy experience. It incorporates references to the Celtic myth of the Children of Lir, where seven brothers were turned into swans, who could only be rescued by their sister, if she spun and wove each of them a shirt of nettles. When they returned, for a single day, she had finished all seven, except the sleeve of her youngest brother's shirt. As she threw the shirts over them, all were transformed back to human form, except the youngest, who still had one wing instead of an arm. Perhaps this means that some people are never really settled.
The backdrop shows the constellations of stars that birds use to navigate in migration.

2009

Glass – 26cm h x 165cm w

Optical glass, sandblast and wheel-engraved, LED light with dichroic colour. Painted textile

Photos: Robin Morton

FLIGHTPATH details

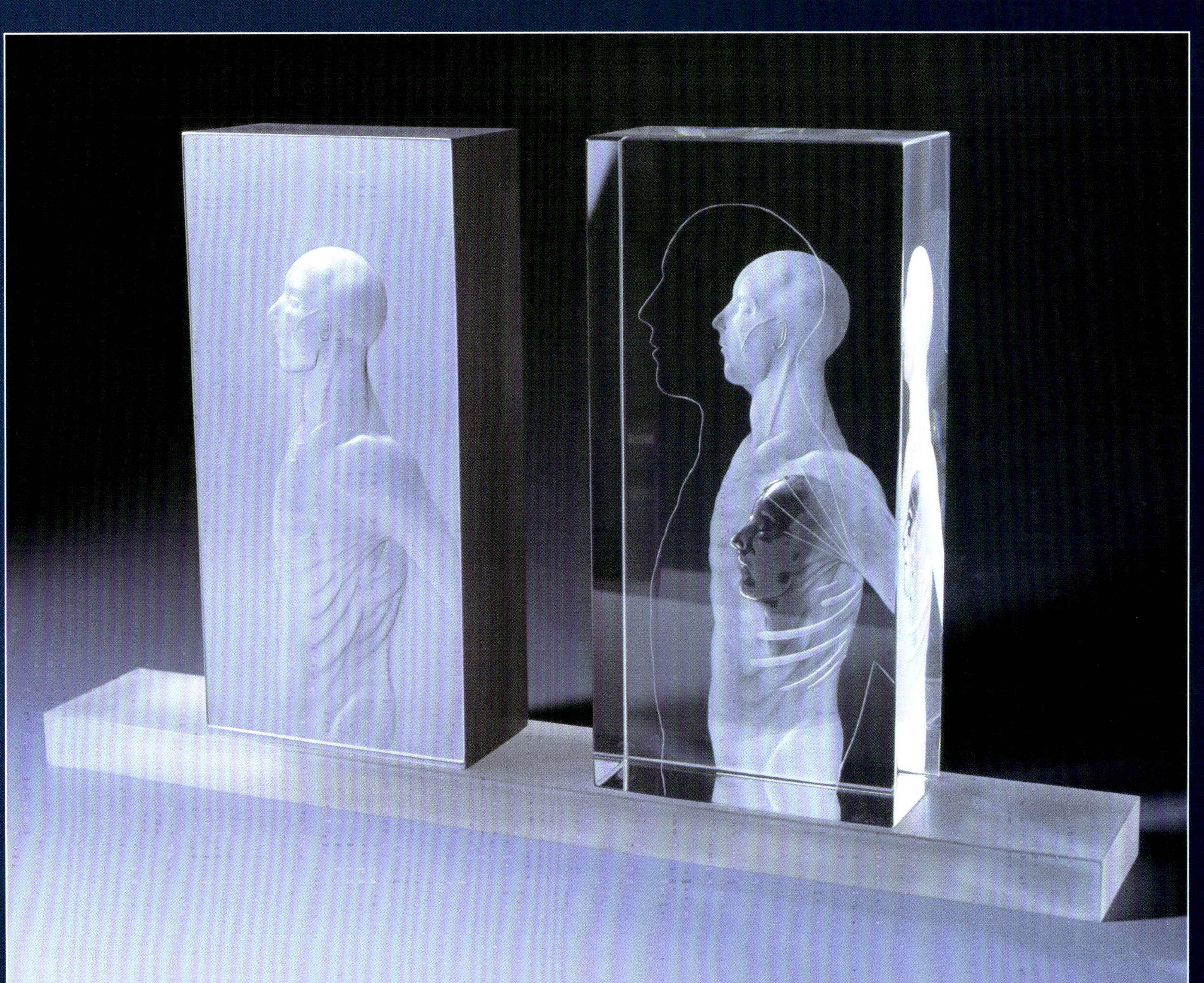

GLASS - FRAGILE

The contrast between the two media is the important focus of this piece. The resin block is cast from the engraving, and provides the same image in relief. It uses sintered aluminium to resemble cast metal, contrasting the solid, machine-like figure with the vulnerability of the transparent engraved glass.

2005

22cm h x 38cm w x 6cm d

*Optical glass, cast resin
Wheel-engraved*

Private Collection

Photo: Ken Smith

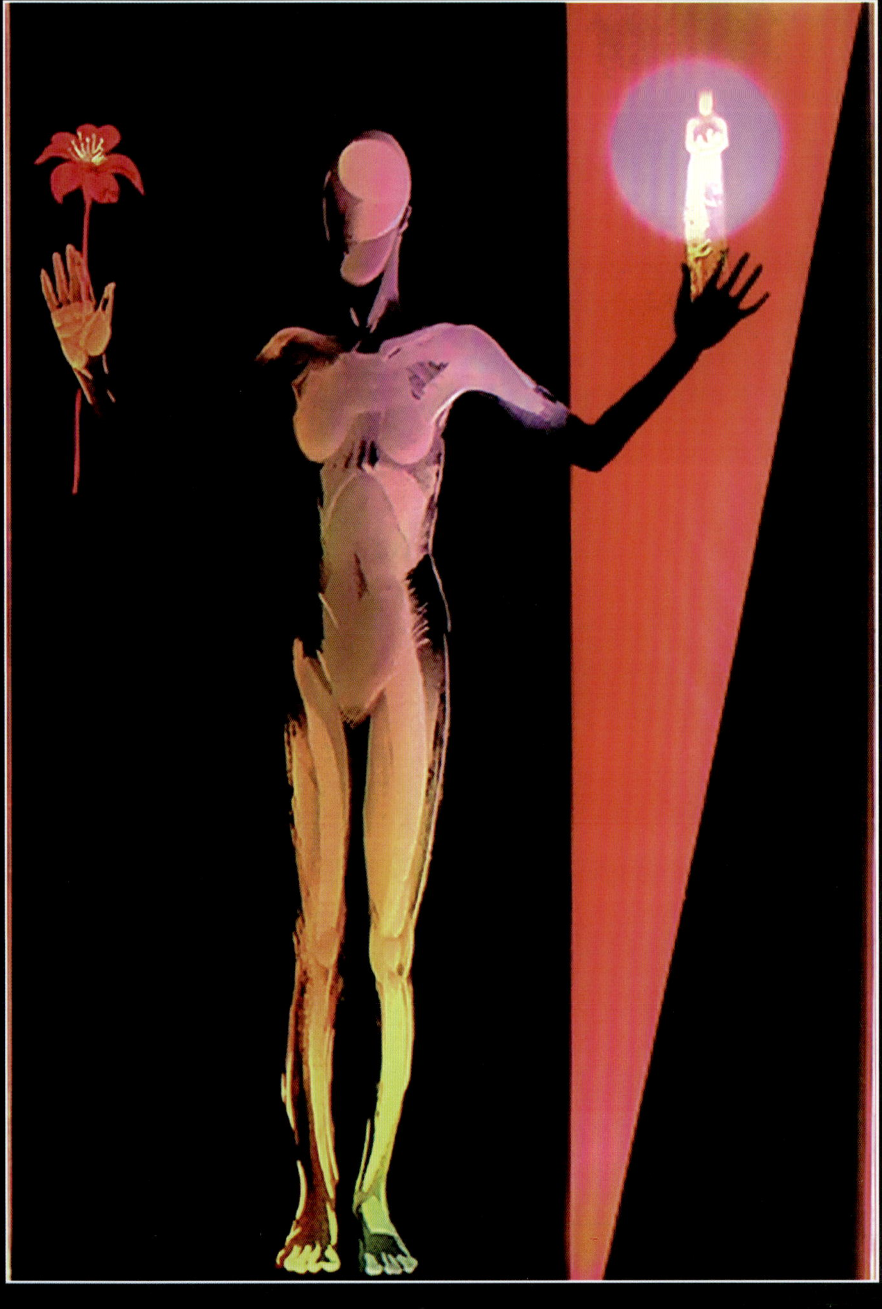

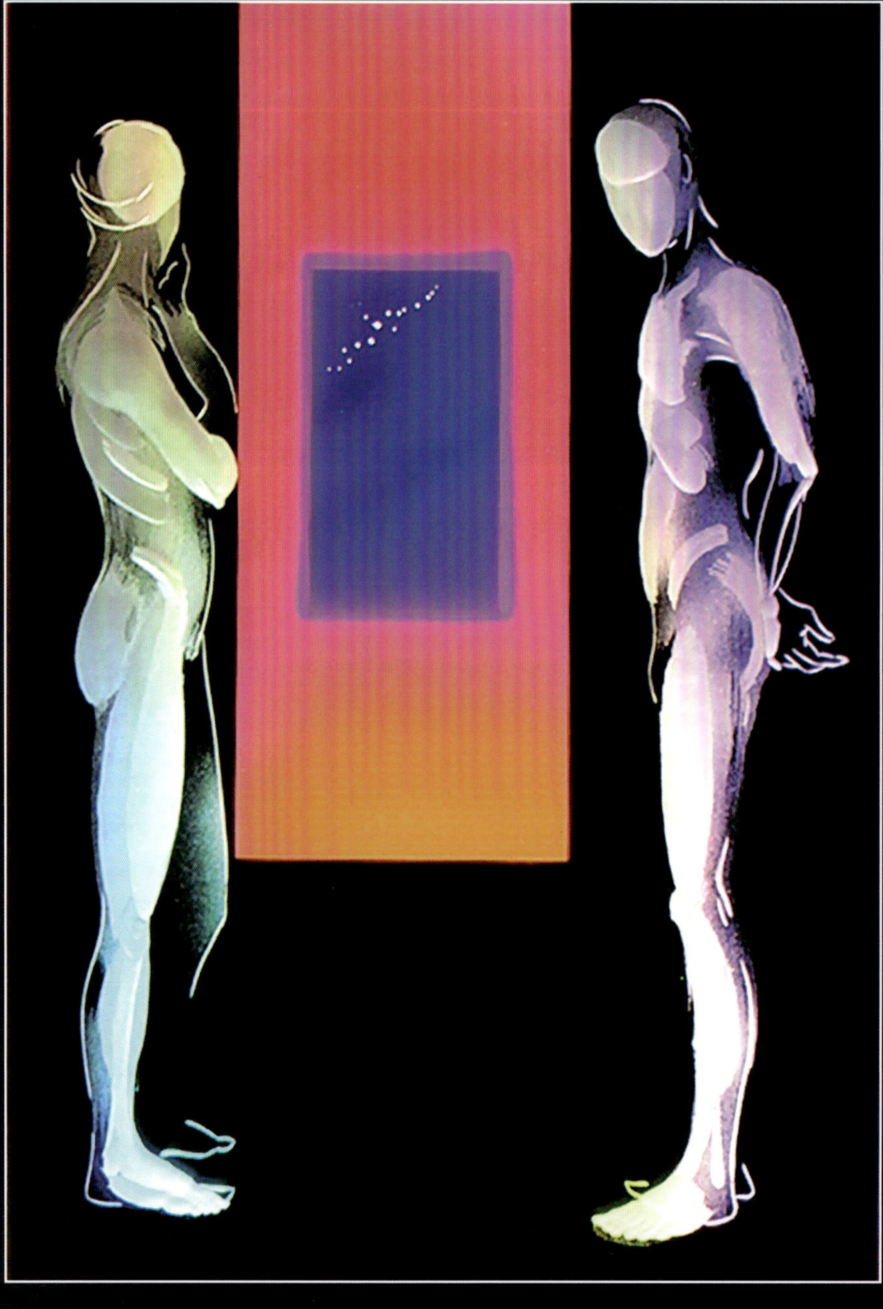

INTERFACE details

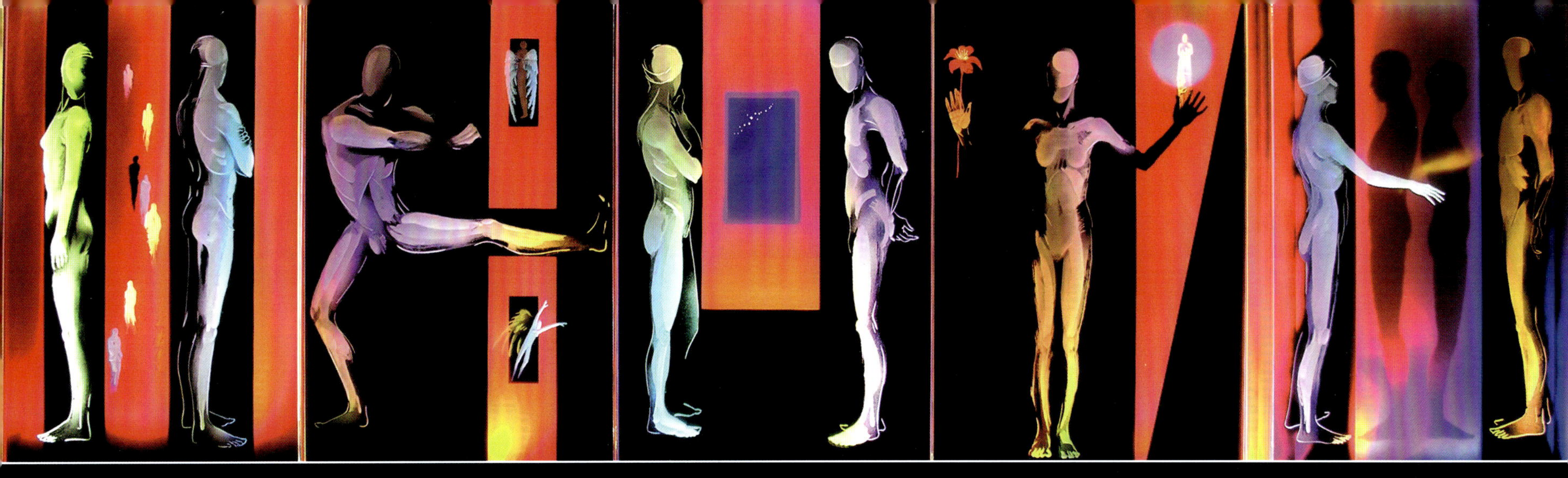

INTERFACE

2007

The North-west United States are known as a centre of art glass activity.
When the owners of the Murano Hotel in Tacoma, remodelled the building,
they decided to focus on this, and commissioned around 40 international
artists to make pieces specially for the hotel, which was designed around
these artworks. Every space shows outstanding glass, beautifully displayed.
It is like a live-in glass museum. Interface speaks about the relationships
between people as they take part in the shifting population of a hotel.

50cm h x 130cm w

Optical glass, sandblast and wheel-engraved

LED lighting with dichroic colour

Commissioned for the Murano Hotel, Tacoma, WA, USA

Photos: Robin Morton

"Alison Kinnaird's skill as an engraver is always at the heart of her work with glass. But she never tires of looking for ways to extend the art of engraving and is not afraid of innovation. On the contrary, her willingness to experiment and to bring new ideas to the field, sometimes by building on an older tradition, sometimes by experimenting with new technology, is what has brought her to prominence."

DAN KLEIN,
THE SCOTTISH GALLERY EXHIBITION CATALOGUE 2004

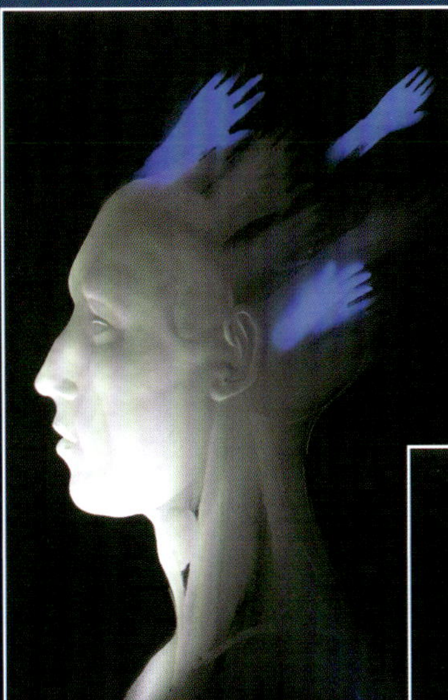

CRAFTSMAN
The brilliantly coloured flickering hands which appear and disappear represent the creative mind.

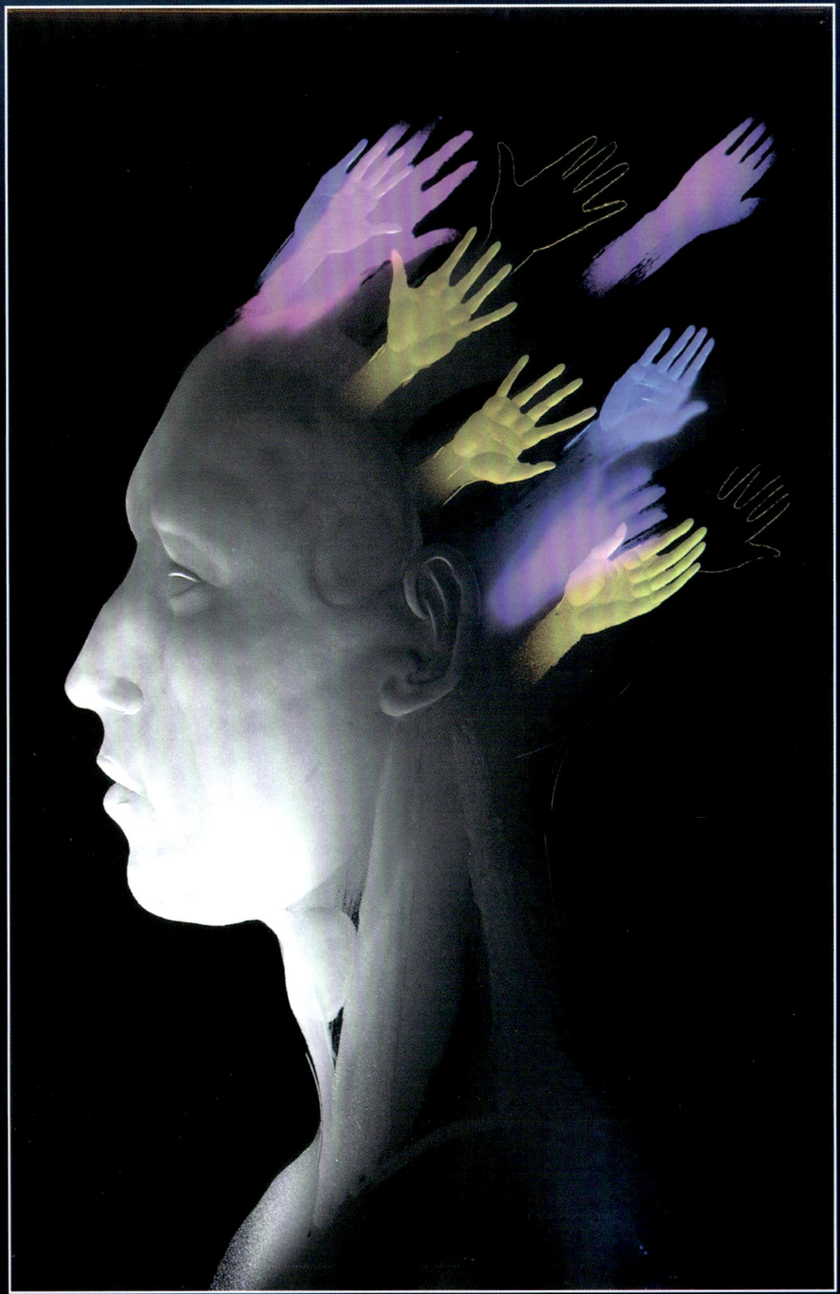

2011

50cm h x 26cm w x 5cm d

Optical glass, sandblast and wheel-engraved, LED lighting with dichroic colour and programmed sequence

Private Collection

Photo: Robin Morton

WHITE LIES

The white block, which is cast off the engraving, shows a figure which appears to be simple, direct and truthful. The contrasting clear block shows that there is much more going on in the background – the small figures which issue from the mouths of the larger engraved and polished forms are scattered down across the black base. Glass is a deceptive medium.

2001

Optical glass, white and black resin

25cm h x 20cm w x 18cm d

Crafts Council Collection

Photo: Ken Smith

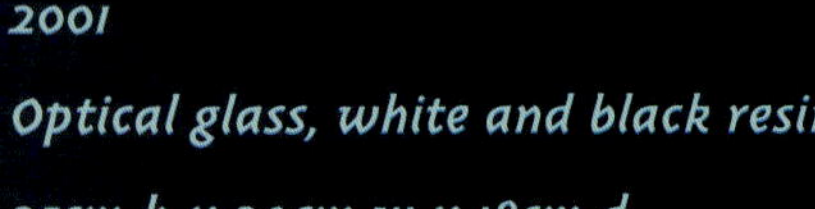

TRUTH

An Egyptian myth told how, to enter the Afterlife, the Soul would be weighed against the Feather of Truth. Glass, with its ambiguous weightlessness, seemed an ideal medium in which to explore this idea.

1985

15cm diameter

Lead crystal, wheel-engraved

Private Collection

Photo: Ken Smith

MIDNIGHT

2010

40cm h x 40cm w

Optical glass, sandblast and wheel-engraved,
LED lighting with dichroic colour

Private Collection

Photo: Robin Morton

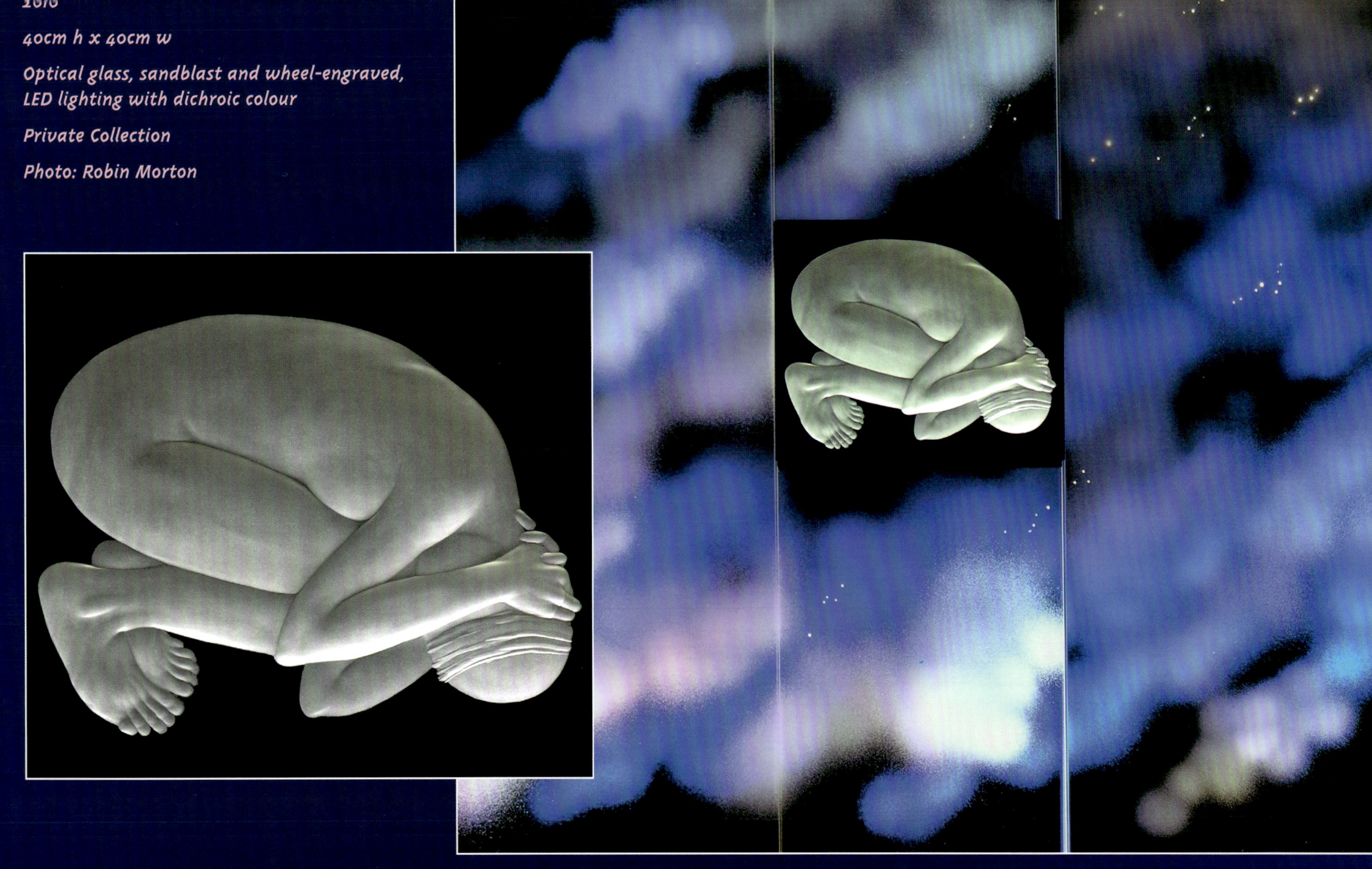

EVOLVE

This installation was a Millenium Commission from Broadfield House. It represents the strata of this coal-mining area and the way in which geology preserves signs of evolution, but it is also a practical demonstration of how intaglio wheel-engraving is done, starting with the basic simple shapes, and working over these to create the form and model the detail.

2000

50cm h x 12cm w x 7cm d

Optical glass, wheel-engraved,
black resin cast off the engraved glass,
steel mount

Broadfield House Glass Museum, Dudley

Photo: Ken Smith

BUTTERFLIES

The butterfly has great significance as a symbol of the soul. These panels show the life-cycle of the butterfly, incorporating tiny human figures in a number of places. The silhouetted 'collection' of butterflies also represent the crucifixion. The caterpillar hanging from a thread represents the fragility and tenuousness of life, while the butterflies bursting from the chrysalis symbolise reincarnation and the soul being drawn toward enlightenment. The reverse side of the panels start with one butterfly, multiplying into many, signifying the church's role as a gathering place.

2005

26cm h x 600cm w

Optical glass, sandblast and wheel-engraved, LED light with dichroic colour

Commissioned by Marchmont St. Giles Church, Edinburgh

The reverse panels donated by Margaret and Alison Kinnaird
in memory of John Kinnaird

Photos: Robin Morton

BUTTERFLIES details

THE PRAISE WINDOW details

THE PRAISE WINDOW – DORNOCH CATHEDRAL

This window was commissioned by his family, in memory of Stuart Anderson, for many years the choir-master and organist of the ancient Cathedral. The figure, with its arms raised in praise, looks out from the Cathedral. It stands on curved lines which represent both staves of music, and rainbows. Down each side and at the foot are choirs of singers and musicians. When I had designed and engraved the glass, the window was assembled and installed by Patrick Ross-Smith from Shetland, with whom I have successfully worked on a number of stained-glass projects.

2005

5m h x 1m w

Flashed glass, sandblast and wheel-engraved, lenses, leaded.

Photos: Robin Morton

NEW CLOTHES

I have often used garment-shaped
pieces of glass as a canvas which
I can fill with symbolic imagery,
with the jewel-like detail that is so
characteristic of wheel-engraving.

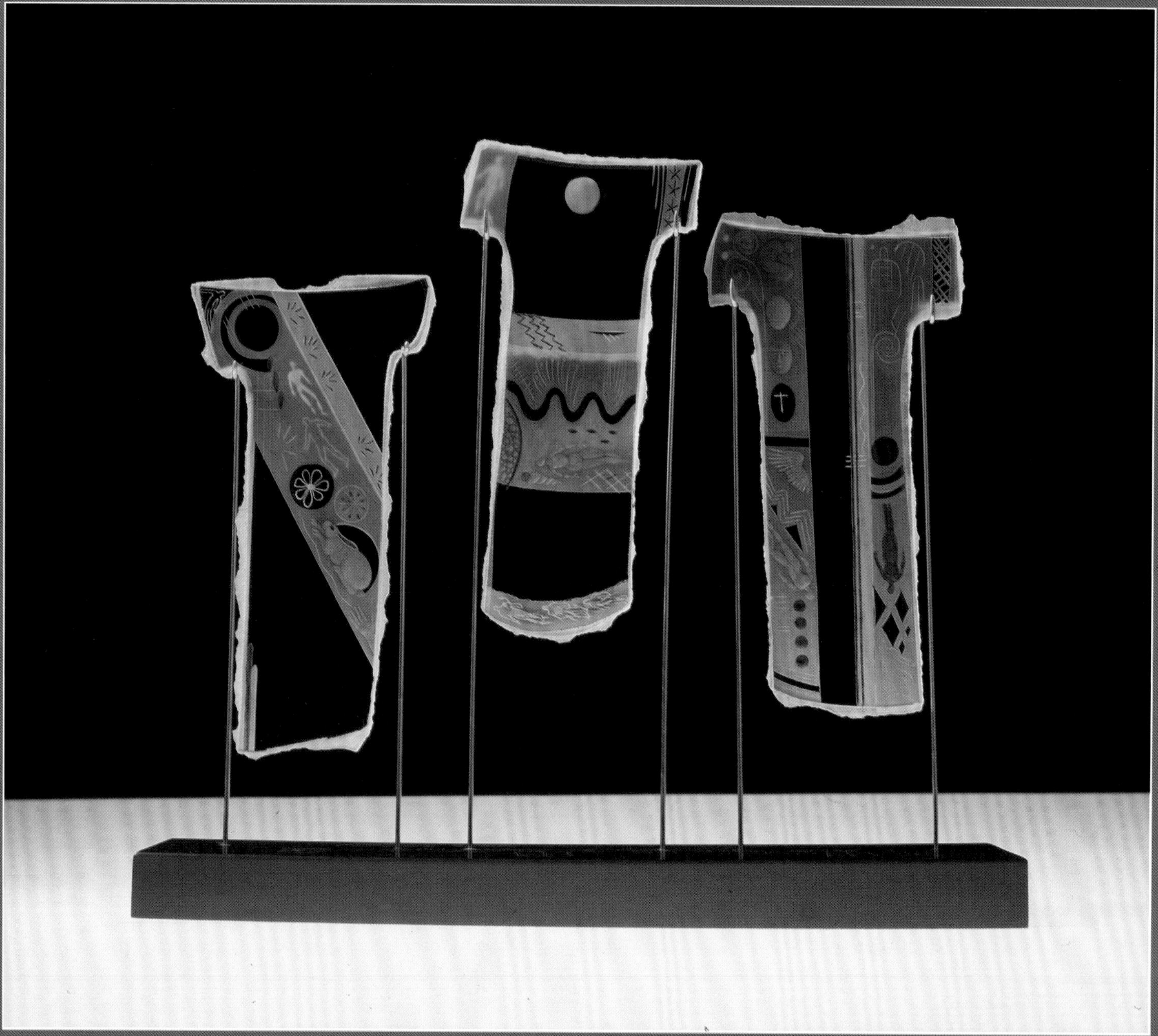

2004

35cm h x 42cm w x 10cm d

Lead crystal, sandblast cut and
wheel-engraved Steel and resin
mount

Private Collection

Photo: Ken Smith

VEIL I & II
These two panels refer to the classical tradition of cameo engraving, through different coloured layers of glass.

2012

each 26cm h x 13cm w

Fused cameo glass
Wheel-engraved

Private Collection

Photo: Robin Morton

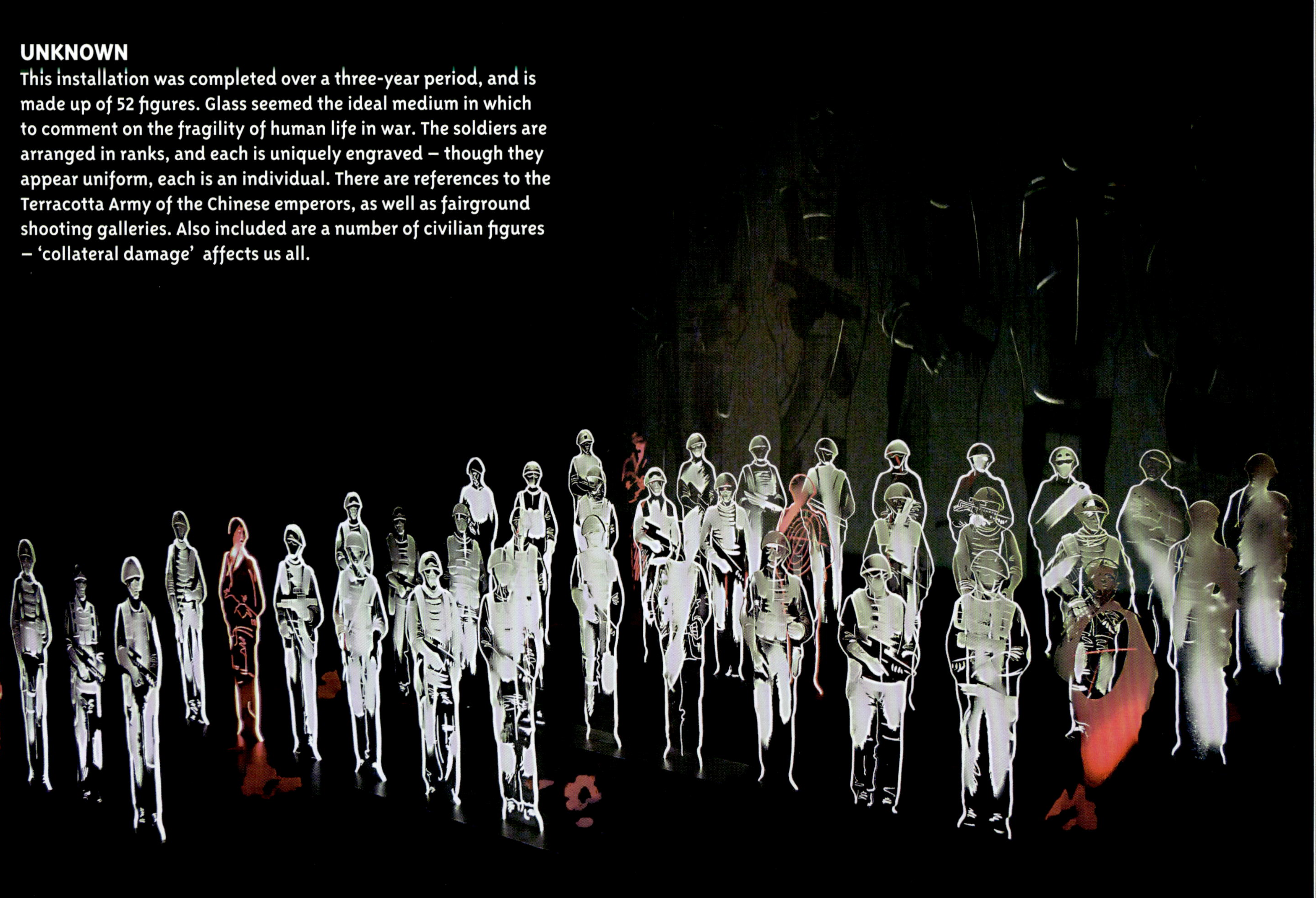

UNKNOWN
This installation was completed over a three-year period, and is
made up of 52 figures. Glass seemed the ideal medium in which
to comment on the fragility of human life in war. The soldiers are
arranged in ranks, and each is uniquely engraved — though they
appear uniform, each is an individual. There are references to the
Terracotta Army of the Chinese emperors, as well as fairground
shooting galleries. Also included are a number of civilian figures
— 'collateral damage' affects us all.

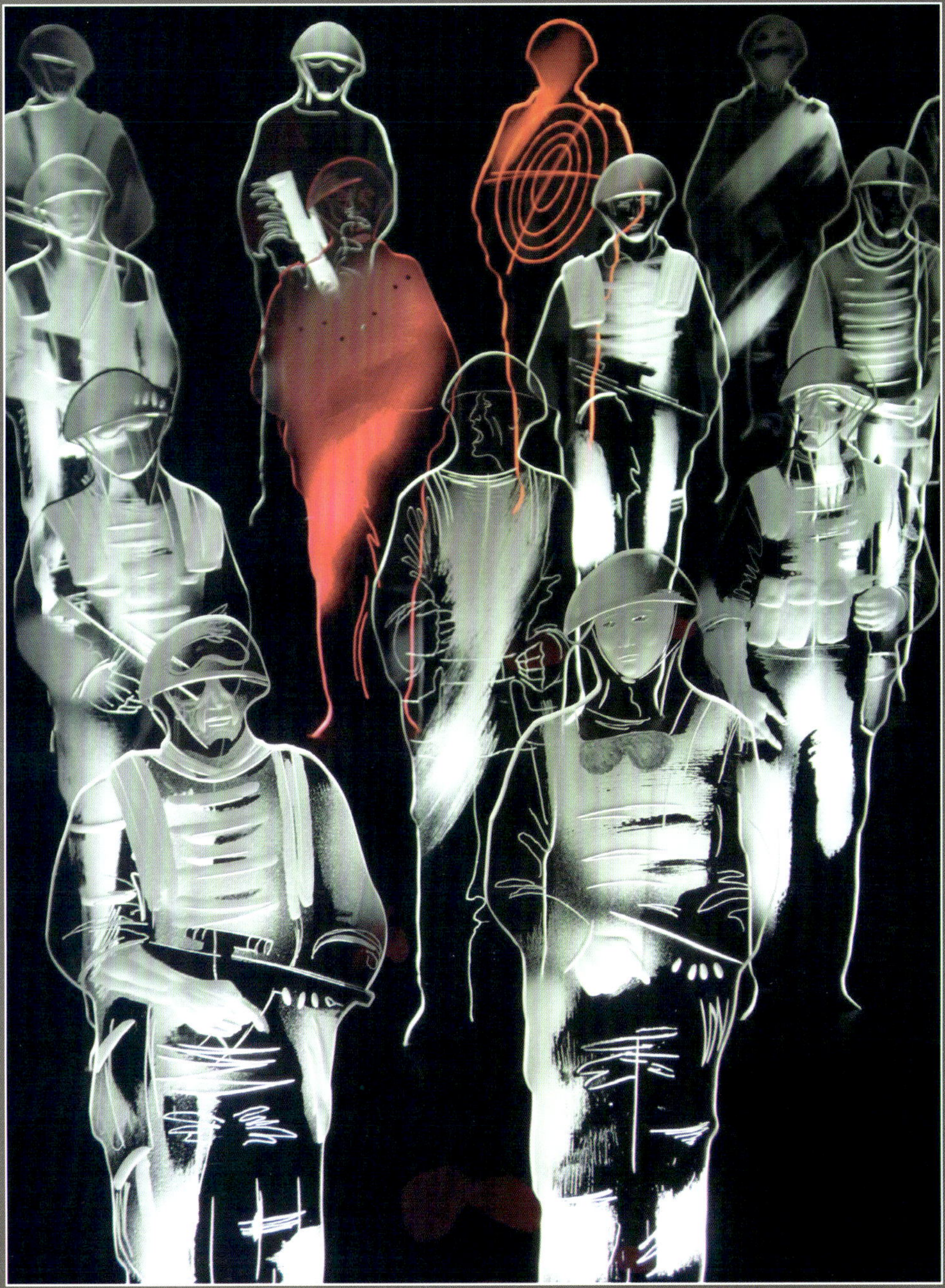

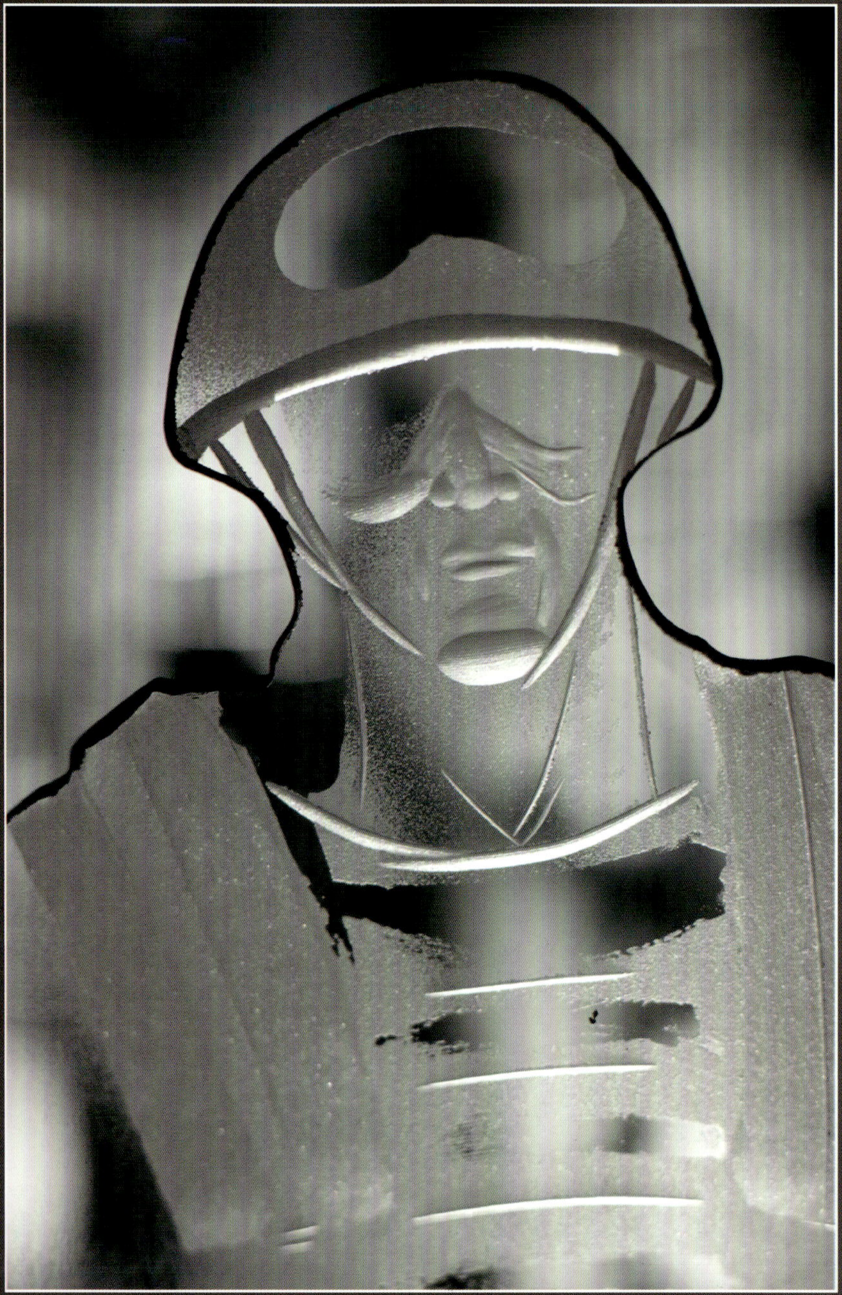

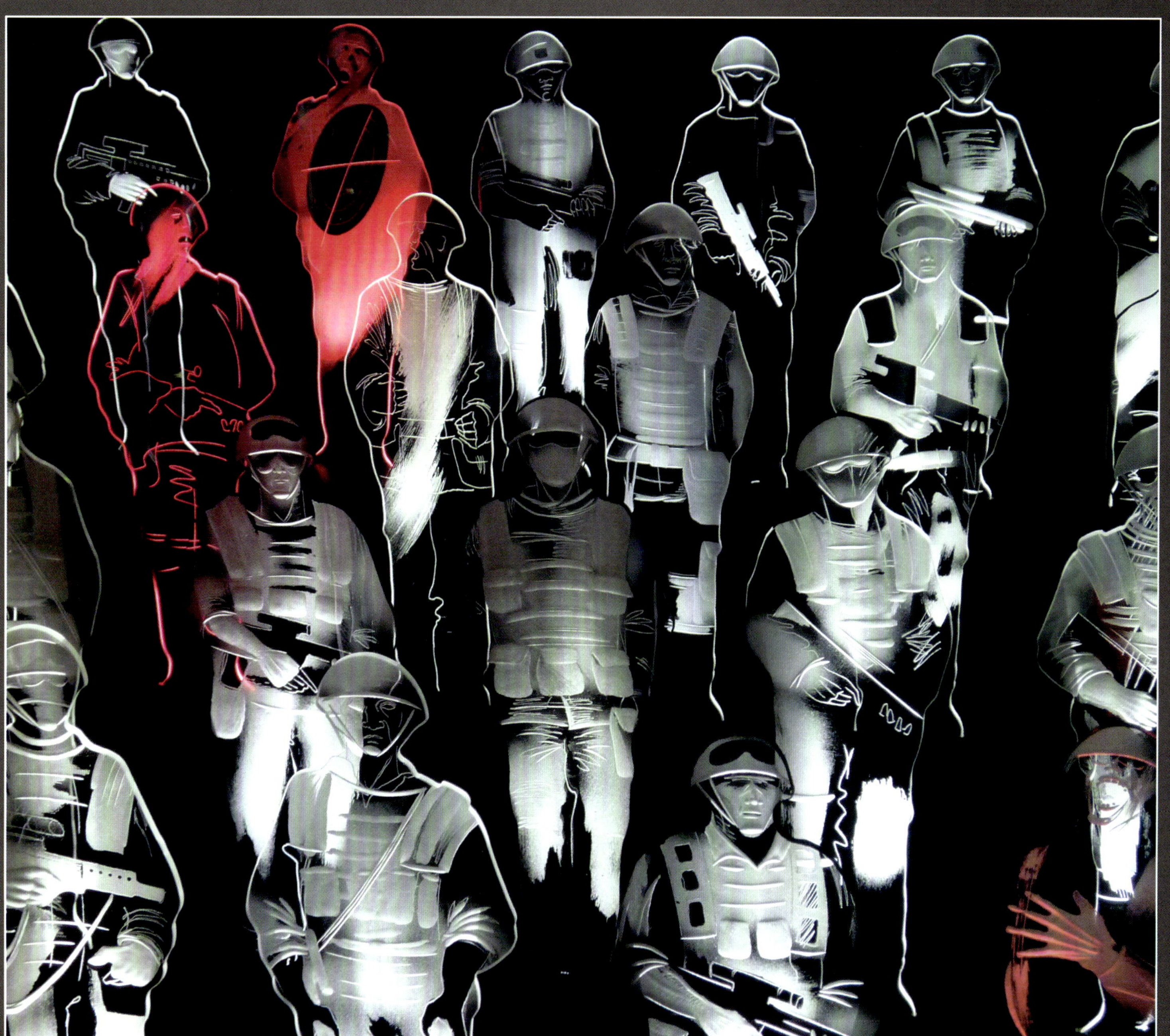

2010 - 2013

50cm h x 190cm w x 190cm d

Optical glass, water-jet cut, sandblast and wheel-engraved, LED lighting, silk poppies, painted textile backdrop

Photos: Robin Morton

FLOWERS OF BUTE

John, Lord Bute, was a great patron of artists and craftsmen, many of whom were invited to make work for his wonderful home, Mount Stuart, on the Isle of Bute. This series of panels were commissioned for a screen in his office. One of his ancestors was a noted botanist, and the subject of the flowers of Bute was chosen as a tribute to him.

1989

each 27cm h x 21cm w

Lead crystal, copper-wheel engraved

Mount Stuart, Bute

Photos: Ken Smith

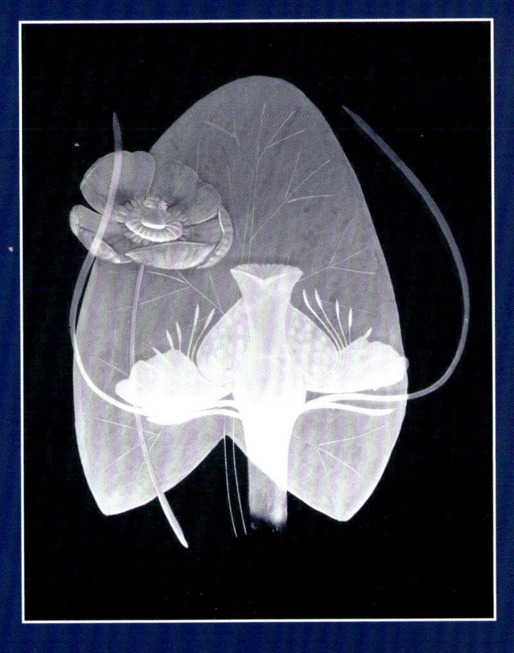

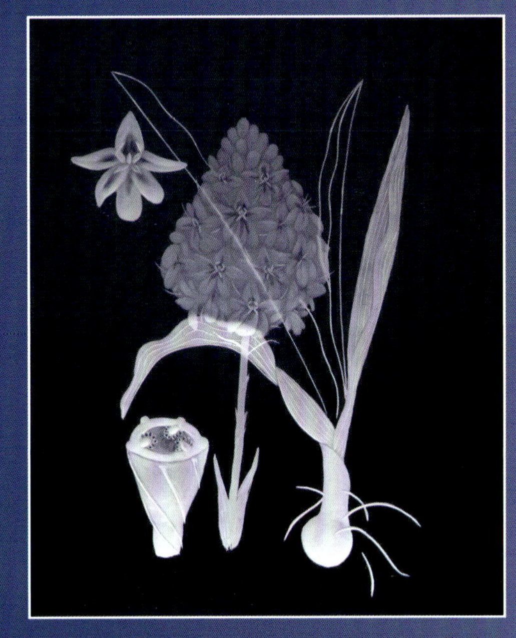

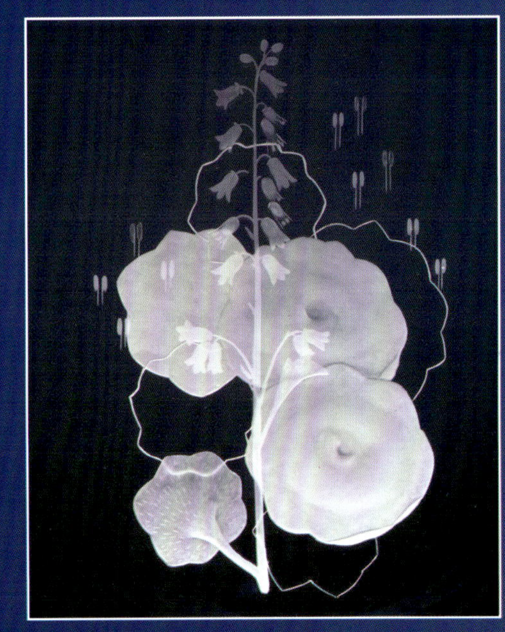

PORTRAIT OF ROY DENNIS

Each year, the Scottish National Portrait Gallery commissions a number of portraits of outstanding Scots. In 2003, the theme was that of nature and conservation. I was commissioned to create a portrait of Roy Dennis, a respected ornithologist who had been instrumental in re-introducing the Sea Eagle and Red Kite to Scotland. I chose to use four layers of glass, allowing me to engrave his profile in decreasing size, which formed a tunnel, down which the engraved birds can fly, suggesting that it is through his imagination that these birds have been restored to our countryside.

2003

50cm h x 20cm w x 15cm d

Optical glass, wheel-engraved and sandblast, oak base, lit

Scottish National Portrait Gallery, Edinburgh

Photos: Ken Smith

Carol Murray

Allan Murray

Walter Nimmo

DONOR WINDOW drawings

THE DONOR WINDOW — SCOTTISH NATIONAL PORTRAIT GALLERY

In 2009, the Scottish National Portrait Gallery closed for a major refurbishment. The contribution of the generous donors was to be recognised in a window. James Holloway, then Director of the Gallery, asked me to create a window which would sit beside the original Victorian sponsors' window, which features the portraits of 24 gentlemen, as well as Queen Victoria. The brief was that the new window should mirror the layout of the original window, and should also continue the botanical theme that runs throughout the decoration of the whole Gallery. The new window includes the portraits of 12 donors, and that of Queen Elizabeth. I chose to offer the corporate donors and charitable trusts which were also involved, an engraved 'bouquet of thanks', featuring flowers that they chose to represent themselves. Each of the individual sitters also chose a flower to surround their portrait — many of these were symbolic, or had particular personal significance. After a number of sittings with each subject, which resulted in detailed drawings, I developed an innovative technique for the portraits, engraving on both sides of flashed glass — glass specially blown with a layer of colour on one side - to give both modelling and highlights, so that the likeness stands out, even at a distance. The Scottish Government and the Heritage Lottery Fund were represented by heraldic roundels. The blue-green background shows a drift of small abstracted figures from the top, down across the entire window, and represent the people of Scotland, since a great deal of public money was involved, and it is a Gallery for the whole nation. Patrick Ross-Smith again worked with me on this major project, sourcing the beautiful colours of glass, cutting the pieces of glass to my design, ready for me to engrave, and assembling and installing the window, before its formal opening by HM Queen Elizabeth in July 2012. This event celebrated the completion of the Gallery's renovation.

2012

3m h x 1.40m w

Flashed glass, wheel-engraved and sandblast

Scottish National Portrait Gallery, Edinburgh

Photos: Robin Morton

DONOR WINDOW details

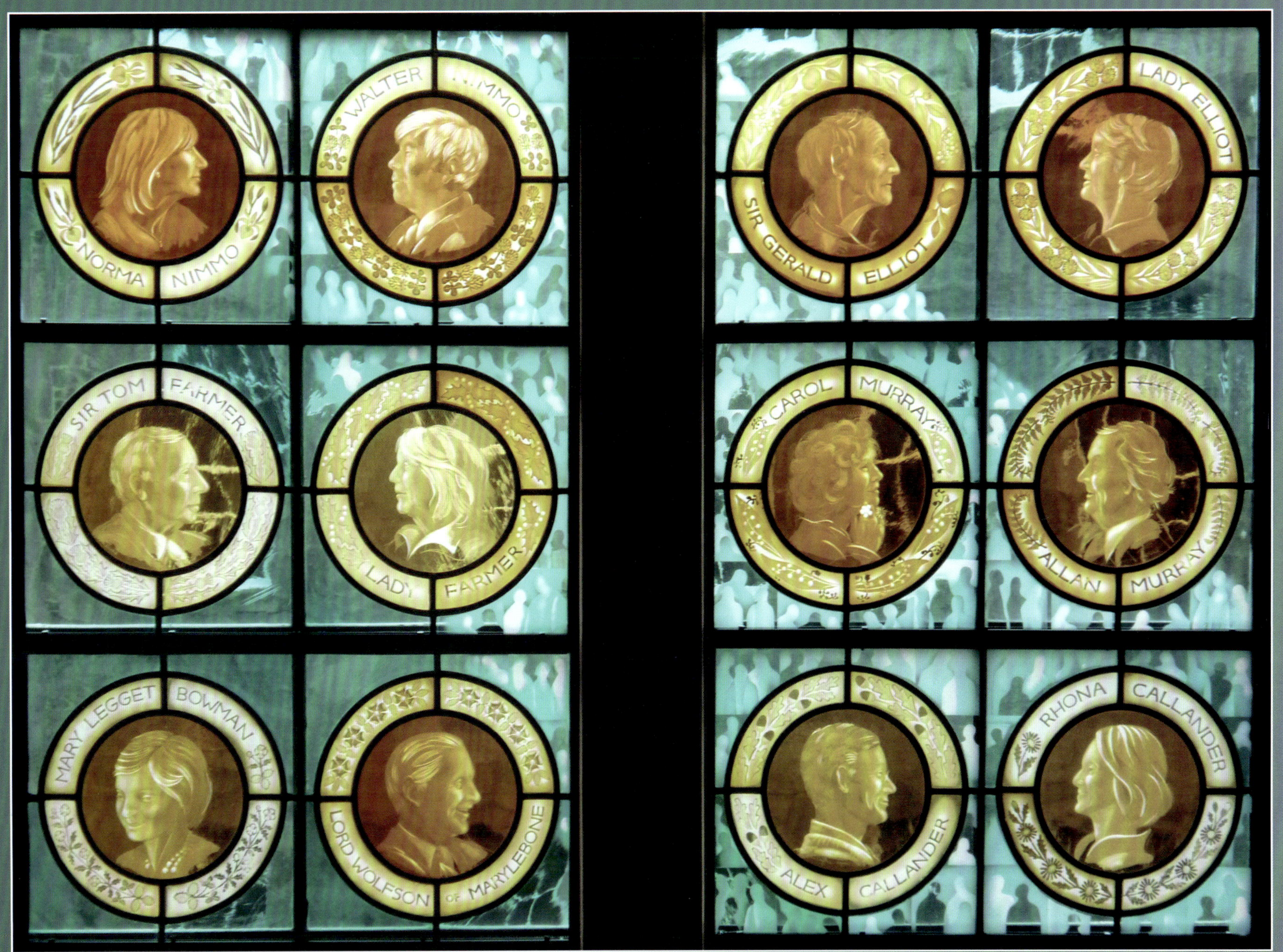
NORMA NIMMO
WALTER NIMMO
SIR GERALD ELLIOT
LADY ELLIOT
SIR TOM FARMER
LADY FARMER
CAROL MURRAY
ALLAN MURRAY
MARY LEGGET BOWMAN
LORD WOLFSON OF MARYLEBONE
ALEX CALLANDER
RHONA CALLANDER

ALEX CALLANDER
RHONA CALLANDER

DONOR WINDOW details

Photo of Portrait of HM the Queen:
Vivian Ross-Smith

ICARUS

This piece is not a literal representation of the classical myth, but symbolises the artist's imagination in flight. The gently flickering wings light up in sequence at random.

2012

50cm h x 30cm w x 15cm d

Optical glass, sandblast and wheel-engraved, LED light with dichroic colour and moving programmed sequence

Photo: Robin Morton

ALISON KINNAIRD MBE MA FGE

www.alisonkinnaird.com

1949   Edinburgh, Scotland

AWARDS

2010   MG Alba Scots Traditional Music Awards, Hall of Fame
2004   Glass Sellers Award
2002   Creative Scotland Award
2001   Adrian Sassoon Award
1998   CC Chelsea First Exhibitors Award
1998   Inches Carr Crafts Bursary
1997   MBE for services to art and music
1987   Glass Sellers Award
1980   SDA/CCC Crafts Fellowship

MEMBERSHIPS

Member of the award panel for Creative Scotland Award 2003-2004
Scottish Arts Council Crafts Committee 1993-1996
Fellow of the Guild of Glass Engravers
BBC Broadcasting Council for Scotland 1984-1987
Contemporary Glass Society
Glass Art Society
Scottish Glass Society
Index of Selected Makers, Crafts Council

TEACHING

Masterclasses, International Festival of Glass, Stourbridge, England
Urban Glass, Brooklyn, NY
College of Art and Design, Wroclaw, Poland
Northlands Creative Glass, Scotland
Corning Glass Studio, Corning NY, USA
Frauenau, Germany

SELECTED EXHIBITIONS

2013   Solo Exhibition, Edinburgh International Fringe Festival
2013   Johansfors, Sweden
2012   Solo Exhibition, 'Luminesce', Linlithgow, Scotland
2012   Fleming Collection, London
2012   Solo exhibition, The Scottish Gallery, Edinburgh
2012   Travelling exhibition, Wroclaw, Jelenia Gora, Ostrow, Lesno, Poland
2010   British Glass Biennale, Invited Artist
2009   UrbanGlass, New York
2008   The Cutting Edge, Royal Museums Of Scotland
2007   Invited Artist, Visual Arts, Scotland, Royal Scottish Academy
2006   British Glass Biennale
2006   Coburg Glaspreis Exhibition, Germany
2006   Glasmuseet Ebeltoft, Denmark
2005   21st Century British Glass, London
2004   Psalmsong, V&A London Museum, London
2004   British Glass Biennale, Stourbridge
2004   Broadfield House Glass Museum, Dudley
2002   Art for Europe, Brussels
2001   Art Glass Gallery, Santa Fe
1999   Kaminesky Senov, Czech Republic
1999   National Glass Centre, Sunderland
1998   Contemporary Applied Arts, London
1996   British Glass, Prague
1996   Contemporary Arts Centre, Utrecht
1988   Solo Exhibition, Coleridge, London
1987   Group Exhibition, Gallery Galerie de Vier Linden, Asperen, The Netherlands
1984   Group Exhibition, Habatat Gallery, Detroit, USA
1979   The Bowl, British Crafts Centre, London, organised by World Crafts Council
1977   Salzburg Festival, Art Gallery, Salzburg, Austria
1975   Contemporary Scottish Artists, Exhibition Centre Edinburgh

SELECTED COLLECTIONS

2012   Standing Feathers, Aberdeen Art Gallery & Museum
2010   Adam and Eve, Shipley Art Gallery, Gateshead
2008   Maze, Royal Museums of Scotland
2005   Psalmsong, Scottish Parliament, Edinburgh
2005   Streetwise I, Tutsek Foundation, Munich
2005   Streetwise II, Dundee Museum & Art Gallery, Dundee
2003   Portrait of Roy Dennis, National Portrait Gallery of Scotland
2001   Evolve, Broadfield House Glass Museum
2001   White Lies, Crafts Council Collection
1995   Triptych, Victoria and Albert Museum, London
1989   Man into Seal, Corning Museum of Glass, New York, USA
1988   Ring of Crystal, Ring of Stone, Leicestershire Museum and Art Gallery, Leicester
1987   Disc - Leap, Ulster Museum, Belfast 1986 Doors on the Past, Royal Museum of Scotland
1986   Disc - She is Summer, Kelvingrove Museum and Art Gallery, Glasgow
1980   Doors - engraved block, Scottish Development Agency
        - Scottish Crafts Collection, Edinburgh

SELECTED COMMISSIONS

2013   Windows, Dornoch Cathedral
2012   Scottish National Portrait Gallery (Donor Window)
2009   Self Portrait, Fitzwilliam Museum, Cambridge
2007   Interface-Panels for Murano Hotel, Tacoma USA
2006   Butterfly panels, Marchmont St Giles Church, Edinburgh
2004   Praise Window, Dornoch Cathedral
2003   Portrait for National Portrait Gallery of Scotland — Roy Dennis
2000   Millennium Commission, Broadfield House Glass Museum
1993   British Film Institute Awards
1992   Door panels, commissioned by Lord Bute of Mount Stuart
1991   Alumnus of the Year Award, commissioned by Edinburgh University
1990   Gift for his Imperial Highness, the Crown Prince of Japan,
        commissioned by Royal Bank of Scotland
1989   Screen of 10 panels, commissioned by Lord Bute of Mount Stuart
1986   Gift for HM The Queen Mother, commissioned by Royal College of Physicians

1983   Duke of Edinburgh Design Award
1980   Wedding bowl for HRH The Prince of Wales,
        commissioned by The Scotsman newspaper
1979   The Wealth of Nations presented to the Institute of Bankers in England,
        commissioned by Institute of Bankers in Scotland

BOOKS

2011   Life story recorded for BRITISH LIBRARY 'CRAFTS LIVES' series
2011   PORTRAIT OF THE NATION, Trustees of the Scottish National Galleries
2008   20th CENTURY BRITISH GLASS, Charles Hajdamach, Antique Collectors Club
2007   Invited Contributor, V & A MUSEUM, 150th ANNIVERSARY CELEBRATION ALBUM
2005   25 YEARS OF NEW GLASS REVIEW, The Corning Museum of Glass
2003   CONTEMPORARY INTERNATIONAL GLASS, Jennifer Hawkins Opie, V & A Pub.
2002   ARTISTS IN GLASS, Dan Klein, Late Twentieth Century Masters in Glass, Mitchell Beazley
1999   ENGRAVED GLASS, Marilyn & Tom Goodearl, Antique Collectors Club
1996   GLASS ART, Peter Layton, Black/Washington
1984   CRAFTWORK SCOTLAND, Brian Blench, Scottish Development Agency

DISCOGRAPHY AND BIBLIOGRAPHY

2005   The Silver String — Temple Records
1994   MacTalla — Mairidh Gaol is Ceol - Temple Records
1992   The Harper's Land (with Ann Heymann) — Temple Records
1990   The Quiet Tradition (with Christine Primrose) — Temple Records
1988   The Scottish Harp — Temple Records
1988   Music in Trust vol 2 (with Battlefield Band) — Temple Records
1987   Music in Trust vol 1 (with Battlefield Band) — Temple Records
1979   The Harp Key — Temple Records

2002   The North East Collection, Kinmor Music
1996   The Small Harp Tutor, Kinmor Music
1995   The Lothian Collection, Kinmor Music
1992   Tree of Strings (with Keith Sanger), Kinmor Music
1990   The Harp Key, Kinmor Music

RAT RACE

A print from an engraved glass roller, this was created at Urban Glass, Brooklyn, NY. The blank roller was a gift from Edison Zapata, who also assisted with the printing process. A potentially exciting direction for the future. It will be interesting to see where this goes.

2013

35cm h, continuous. Ink on paper.

Photo: Alison Kinnaird

ACKNOWLEDGEMENTS AND CREDITS

Working as an artist can be a rather solitary life, but when one looks outside the studio, there is a huge circle of help, advice and friendship, there as support. The people listed below have all contributed enormously to this book and the work within it, in many ways, over many years.

James Holloway CBE

Jennifer Opie

Dan Klein and Alan J. Poole

Hugh Cheape

Dorota Milkowska

Marta Sienkiewicz

John Slavin

Ewan MacGregor

Denise Lindsay

Ken Smith

Patrick and Vivian Ross-Smith

Nicola Kalinsky

Sir John Leighton

Isabel Anderson

Rev. Susan Brown

David Kaplan and Annica Sandstrom, Lindean Mill Glass

Jane Bruce

Edison Osorio Zapata

Urban Glass

Professor Duncan and Liz Timms

Fiona Andreas, Scottish Parliament Art Collection

Sven Hauschke, Kunstsammlung der Veste Coburg

Adam Aaronson

Michael Bullen

North Lands Creative Glass

The Scottish Gallery

Andrew Draper

Simon Meadows

Tina Norris

Simon Hollington

Lutz Naumann, Kunstsammlung der Veste Coburg

Margaret Kinnaird

and especially my husband, Robin Morton.

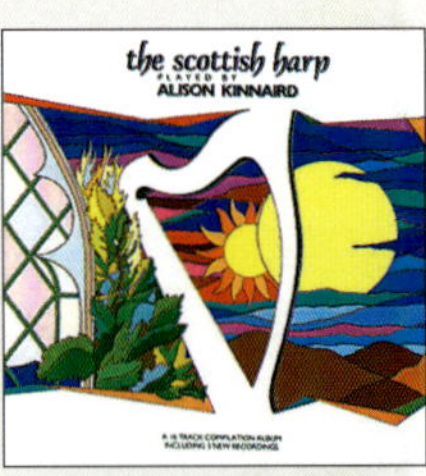
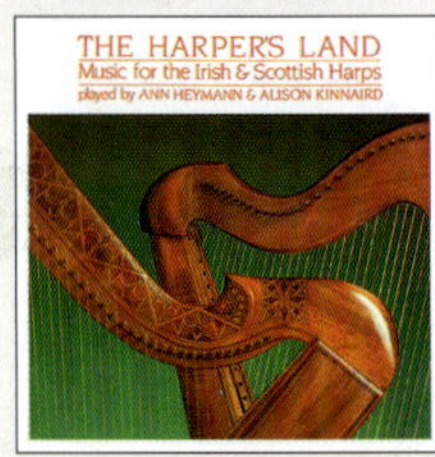

Alison's involvement with Scottish harp music has always run parallel to her art. She played a major part in the revival of the instrument, and is highly respected at home and abroad as a performer, lecturer and teacher. The complementary DVD includes 2 music tracks from her past albums, and 3 short films by Robin Morton which feature the creation of the Donor Window for the Scottish National Portrait Gallery; the making of Psalmsong; and Ring of Crystal, Ring of Stone.

COMPLEMENTARY DVD WITH FILMS & AUDIO TRACKS

FILMS

1. REFLECTIONS...

chapter 1 Portrait of an Artist

chapter 2 Creation of the Donor Window

2. PSALMSONG

chapter 1 Artist's Introduction

chapter 2 Psalmsong Film

3. RING OF CRYSTAL, RING OF STONE

AUDIO TRACKS OF ALISON'S MUSIC

1. ELLEN'S DREAMS

composed by Robin Morton. Pub. Kinmor Music

From 'The Harper's Land' (Temple Records COMD2102), 1992

2. THE BATELL OF HARLOE / THE MARCH OF DONALD, LORD OF THE ISLES, TO THE BATTLE OF HARLAW

(featuring Alasdair White on fiddle & whistle)

trad. arr. Alison Kinnaird & Alasdair White

From 'The Silver String' (Temple Records COMD2096), 2004